750

SHINE ON

SHINE ON

Stories by
Fred Pfeil

LHP

Acknowledgements

Some of the stories here enclosed have appeared in the following journals: *Boston University Journal*, *The Minnesota Review*, *Mississippi Mud*, *Ploughshares*, *The Sewanee Review*, *Spectrum*, *Story Quarterly*.

"The Quality of Light in Maine" also appeared in *The O'Henry Awards, Prize Stories, 1979* (Doubleday), New York, 1979.

Publication of this book was made possible in part with the support of the Massachusetts Council on the Arts & Humanities, a State agency whose funds are appropriated by the Legislature and approved by the Governor.

Lynx House Press books are distributed by Small Press Distribution, 1814 San Pablo Avenue, Berkeley, California 94702; and by Bee Line Distribution, Box 339, Burton, Washington 98013.

Library of Congress Cataloging in Publication Data
Pfeil, Fred
    Shine On

    Contents: Shine On — Skeeter's Last Reflection — Night Game — Poker Fugue — The Fame of Price — Miss Olive's Retreat — The Quality of Light in Maine — The Collected Works of Brown — Holding On
    I. Title.
PS3566.F45S5 1986   813'.54   86-3009
ISBN 0-89924-047-X

Cover art by Tom Prochaska.
Author's photo by Line Kesler.

This small book has a large dedication.
It goes to the memory of my grandfather and strong namesake, Fred Herriman; to my grandmother, Nell Herriman, indomitable and beloved; and to my parents, Bob and Harriet, who have stood beside me all this time.

Contents

Shine On

Shine on
Oh let it shine on
Let your light from the lighthouse
Shine on me
     —Traditional gospel song

Evening; late July, 1968

Thinking, seeing still the body of Steven Ketchum, the picture of it floating behind his eyes, Carl Aldred slides the steel door of his new-built garage open. Behind him, the sun over the dipping round hills at the west edge of town flows a thick orange. Carl steps away from its last light, takes no notice of the gloss the sun strikes on the green-painted ribbed steel, the same way anybody tends not to notice such things when they're in a hurry. And he is in a hurry; it's getting late.

What does catch his eye, fills it in fact, are the two yellow school buses on either side of him; but he doesn't look straight at them just yet. Without thinking it over, looking at them right off still doesn't seem right. Not without some postponement, some—preparation. What he does is walk, thinfaced, long narrow almost sleepy-looking grey eyes turned downwards a little toward the hose on the ground up ahead, so he sees those buses just as dusky gold lumps pressing the sides of his sight. It is pretty dark in here, no windows, the only light coming in from outside, barely through the door. Turning the light on in here will wait for a while too.

At the back end of the garage he stoops down to pick up the hose, the special hose he bought. Moves almost hurriedly for it; a little more and it would be a snatch. That boy, that Steven Ketchum, still floats in his head.

No. Not boy. The body, the boy's body. The corpse. (*Corpse* being the word Halpern always uses when he, Carl, brings them in in the gleaming Lincoln, and he and Halpern carry them downstairs. The downstairs word, though, just for the basement where Halpern works on them; upstairs, so far as he knows, it's usually put as the remains.)

3

Black and blue the kid's face was; his whole body, actually. Dark pitch purple, color of tar, shading into color of violets some places. Like he was bruised all over. Like every place on you you could fall, Steve Ketchum had fallen hard. (Two days, Halpern said, mad, shaking his head. Two days anyway, monoxide to boot. Sweet jumping Jesus Christ, Halpern said. Sweat was on his forehead's edge, gleaming. And those poor simple bastards want him presentable.)

Black and blue: all over. And the smell that came out . . .

Easily thick as his own boy Danny's wrist is the black hose. A special outfit from Sears; it's a double hose actually, with a gun-end nozzle practically as big as the Lugers Carl remembers folks bringing back from the war when he was a kid. Has regular triggers on it, two of them, one just for water, the other running back to a cylinder of detergent the same size and shape as an acetylene tank, dark green in the corner, to shoot the soap. Quite a rig in all.

But taking hold of it and aiming at the ground still isn't quite enough to relieve him; somehow, he feels still troubled in a way he can no more get away from than grab onto. Maybe even more so now since he's noticed that about Danny and the hose. With the other so fresh in his mind (Carl, listen, could you give me a hand with this just for an hour or so? Halpern said. I know you don't like it and it's not your job but I'll give you some extra for it, and Jesus Christ . . .) what's happened, in effect, is that back in his mind the worries over whatever's wrong with Danny that's making him act so quiet, you'd even say troubled himself these days—these worries over Danny's trouble fit into that fresh memory, those pictures he's just seen. He knows this rather than thinks it, knows it the same way you know you're in pain: While the soap jets from the silver plastic gunbarrel, hits the ground like spilt milk, foams up then before it sinks and hisses in.

And that knowledge too pools out. Finally Carl lets go of the trigger, too washed with feeling to do anything else for a minute. The feeling's that strong, and large enough, inclusive enough, to be almost outside him, almost something he could know. Starting with this poor dead 16-year-old Steven Ketchum (why dead?), running through and into Danny, soon it has swollen enough to cover just about everyone he knows. But especially his family, wife, son, and daughter, and himself; for them all his worries have run together.

But his last thought was only this: World War Three, Ellie says it is that Danny thinks World War Three is coming and everybody's gonna get killed. (*What it is, whatever Danny says or thinks is eating at him—he might, probably does, have a name and shape for it. And World War Three or A-bomb is as good a one as any. But whatever it is, really, that's eating at him that he hates or fears or just can't stop thinking about it till it makes him sick: it is not what he thinks it is. Not any more than when I would lie awake at night when all I was doing was working at the plant, would lie there by the sleeping body of my wife this woman Ellie and try to figure out how I could get out of there and do what else for a living. Or will lie quite still tonight probably thinking of this boy I've hauled on my buses probably but didn't know, this Stevie Ketchum, with horror and at-traction and sadness and anger because he is willfully dead. Or will lie there openeyed and wonder when Bev will get in from the drive-in with a boy I know is trying to fuck her my daughter. None of this, or of a thousand other things I think, have thought, will think, will be really it.*

Nor do I have a name for it, nor can I think, think more than only that it does not have to do with these things that cover up, confuse, blind what it really is.

But now at this very instant here what it is is so strong it is almost a thought, almost enough to say, to think out loud the words, finally the words—

Sick at heart? No. Not even that, groaned, shouted, sung, would reach the right bones in the right way.

Or that what we all know is this: it's not good being asleep and we don't want to die, but it's not enough the way we are, and where's whatever it feels like we're always just about to find?

On the wings of what beauty, ease, grace?

Just missing. That's all you can say about it. But you know more. Sick at heart, you could say; or say all the rest of this; and that would not be it either.)

That boy. That black body.

(That boy, Stevie, Ketchum, what'd he know of this? How much, enough for it to come fullblown from knowledge to thought? And would that be why he's gone and killed himself? And if so, what else? That maybe he was finishing the knowl-edge with the action? Or, just as likely, running from it, trying to

scratch it out. Or maybe he was just screwed up and knew noth-
ing of this: screwed up over the A-bomb, some girl; some sad
silly thing.)

The body, black as if all the light'd been sucked right out of it.
Worse than usual. Sometimes you brought ones in looking like
they still held light inside them, glowing with it, though pale or
sallow or red-cheeked. Not Ketchum's: lightless, black;
Halpern said that was carbon monoxide for you. Carl held the
shoulders down that Halpern pitched the barbed needle into
like a harpoon, and the body jerked and some gas whooshed out
and the smell . . .

(What was that anyway, what was I, what? . . . ?)

Now Carl's head turns and quickly rises, and he looks out the
garage with his eyes narrowed to spot whatever just happened,
to find the change in things his body shifted, flinched to, told
him of. But nothing has happened. The sun is down now, but
has been since just after he first walked in. Since then the sky has
gone a few shades darker blue. But streetlights haven't come on
yet, and what few birds were singing outside in the maples lin-
ing the street are still going strong.

No, its nothing outside that's happened to make him tense
and look up. He's just come back to himself, that's all. Which is
to say he's forgotten the minute before.

And it's time now to turn on the garage light, a single flood-
light bulb; and, when he does, for it to shine down on those
buses while he puts the soap to them. One by one, moving
smooth and clean, he guides the soapspray around and over
their sides and tops of yellow lined with black and lettered
Boonesboro Jr-Sr High School he first spray-stenciled on their
sides two years ago when he got the loan from the bank and
bought them. Under that bright light those yellows, especially
now they're wet down, positively gleam and sparkle and shine
back at him, and he moves faster and smoother as he goes.

Every Saturday night he does it come hell or high water,
Steven Ketchum or no, washes the dust of those back roads he
and the fellow who drives for him take kids up and back into
those farms in the hills to and from the school five days a week,
every week. You'd miss church before those damn buses'd go
dirty, Ellie said one other time like this when Halpern had called
him out or something had happened to make it late before he
could get to them; but she didn't say it angry. Besides, if you

were to make an issue of it, it's true; and they both know it.

Not that he doesn't believe; both of them, he and Ellie, were brought up to and are making sure the kids are too. Church, though, and this (going over the soap-slick sides with wet rags, rubbing grease and ground-in spots out the spray didn't cut, the corners of his mouth lifted up) are two different things. Church you just go to, sit and listen to—in a way, like paying your respects at somebody's funeral, though that's just because of Ketchum tonight probably that he's thinking that way. The thing about church is, as far as he's concerned, what else can you do except go there, which doesn't take much. Whereas these buses they are what he calls his Big Idea; they got him out of the plant; someday they will let him quit driving ambulance for Halpern when they're all paid up; someday they will have given him so much he won't even have to drive himself; and he will buy more then and they will be his too.

Maybe it is just that it is completely dark out now, and moonless besides, and the streetlights still aren't on; but more probably it is that Carl's eyes are full of his Big Idea. For it pools over him, that warm rich yellow growing brighter and richer every minute under the electric floodlight till his whole dear damn body feels full of the color he loves. By then he is done soaping down the buses. He picks up the hose and rinses them off by pressing on the second trigger of his gun.

*

Just before switching the light off over the sink, a hard bright white lozenge sticking out of the ceiling above and forward from where she stands, Ellie catches sight of something in the window. But no, not quite *in* it. More like in the night outside where it's almost past twilight into dark and shapes start to twist just before disappearing. And like what she sees swims like a fish out of all that, those houses fading and dimming trees: like all that is melting into what this thing like a fish swims out of, transparent but still colored white as paste, as the belly of a fish.

What is it? Her face. Too fat, with flesh that used to top the cheeks down at the bottom now, sagging, like the whole face is sliding down bit by bit off her head. And that might be why there's that wide round funny look in the pouchy eyes which might have been what made her think fish when she caught sight of it in the first place.

She watches her mouth purse. She turns out the light.

Thumb and forefinger of each hand on the side of the dish-towel, she snaps it over to a fold, sending, from the swift roll of the purple and white check cloth, a tiny breeze her way. It hits her in the forehead where small sweat beads sit, fanning them cool and bringing them to her faint notice at the same time, along with the numb band just below her waist from leaning for the last twenty minutes against the sink edge, doing Carl's dish-es and the other supper ones from when the rest of them ate earlier after he got called out. (Carl's face souring on the phone while the rest of them ate.

Found the Ketchum boy, he says from the other side of the kitchen after hanging up. Got to go pick him up.

Dead then? she says, thinking how he looks more sick and mad than usual, and palefaced.

Then Danny, across the table from her, wrinkles up his face, and starts rubbing his hands clenched on the yellow plastic tablecloth; and she looks sharp at him to see if he's doing all right and can handle this; or will it upset him too much, and is not sure what she sees; and turns back again to Carl her hus-band, who she sees doesn't know either.

Suicide I guess, Carl says, his voice not so harsh now and using a special word an eight-year-old, with luck, won't know yet; and turns to go.

I'll keep this here warm for when you're back, she says, and turns back to Danny, worried sick at the table. And thinks how funny it is with all of them feeling so awful, even Bev a little bit now, her young head cocked back looking puzzled like she's just been told a joke or something she doesn't get, and Carl having to go out on a worse-than-usual call when he hates and fears them anyway, and Danny, who gets set off by anything at all nowdays to think on whatever's eating at him that he doesn't tell about, and her too, herself feeling so awful for all of them and for the young boy everybody's been looking for in the hills for the past two days—how funny it is, the way they can all feel so awful and that young boy be dead while there is still shiny day-light spilling through the window on the deep red, cracked lino-leum floor. And shivers.)

There's no question of giving in to that numbness, though, or being done with the day. Because even if there weren't ironing left to do, at least Danny's pants and Carl's suit and a dress for Bev for church tomorrow, and Bev's date to be at the door in just a minute probably, and Danny to come home still from wherever he is riding around town on his bike (thinking what? in terror? fearing his death? all their deaths, the Bomb, or something more, something other, what?), and even though Carl is probably going to fall asleep on the couch with the tv on as soon as he comes up from the garage: it still wouldn't be right, not even then, to give in to sweet rest, to give the jobs and worries up and let things ride. And knowing that for those reasons, all of them, she can't, mustn't let that band of numbness spread before she has put in three more hours of doing and thinking to make it rightly 10:30 has gotten, over the years, to be a sort of pleasure in itself for her. So has the worrying and work itself, her raw material in its way; and she knows it; and, turning into the living room, sighs.

In just the same way she moves away from the lamp she turns on at the endtable by the couch, away from the pool it might throw around her and away from the couch she might have laid down on if she'd given herself half a chance. At the other side of the living room, in the farthest, dimmest reach of the light, the board is up and waiting from earlier between supper and when Carl got back, and the blue washbasket still half-full beside it. On her way over to them, she turns on the Zenith box tv, pointing its pour of silver across the center of the room, confusing the edges of lamplight pool, both lights more or less passing her by; and thinks, Might as well do it all, get it all out of the way, might as well. Almost as if she might ever have considered doing anything else but that in the first place.

At the board she plugs the old Sunbeam in, and waits the first moment of its warming with head bowed down so low chin touches chest. The national news on tv reaches her, passes her mind as smooth as water over rounded stones; the way the words run past and over her, they take her mind off everything else for a minute without latching on themselves. And she knows this is happening, and lets it happen, feeling the heaviness of her head and face released, let go, a rest squeezed in while the Sunbeam heats, an allowable drifting off. (*Just as I am helpless, surrendering to my knowledge that, just as I know—*

No, not

know. Just as I am—

Not even am.

For she has been, is, lost for the

*moment, there is no center, not even to the weakness from the back of
the thighs on down, the scraped hollow bowl inside the stomach, the
whir and hum in the head. Even these are left behind and lost and all
memories of herself and all those in her family that she loves, and the
freshness of that poor boy's death, smear and blur in the motion of her
body and soul in their flight, their streaking, across the space of what
tv screen, living room, town, world?*

> *More like the sky; more like the
dimmest sky; like arching through, hurtling against, deflecting off
the night; and still going. And still going.*

> *Or but is it this soul, this
body, both so fixed and roped and at the board here stuffed with
weight: or something else, something harder to put a finger on, higher
maybe too. Some just plain forcing or flight, some movement only,
which is this now: not just what she knows, or even what she is, but
which fills and runs through and consumes her at these times.*

Something; a shadow moving fast.)

The iron is ready; enough time has gone by. She lifts her head,
picks up the sprinkler bottle to wet down Bev's good pale green
dress, and is, without thinking twice, as conscious as can be, and
back to work. (Madge, says the lady Madge walks with by the
hedge on a bright sunshiny day, I wish I knew what it is that's
making me so tired and cranky nowadays. Carol, Madge says,
Why not do what I do? . . .) Lately, as far as she's concerned,
Bev's heading toward dangerous ground (bending closer for the
pleats in the sleeves, tightening her lips), too proud of herself
and not taking care, plus that boy Larry she goes out with. Any-
body else not her mother would see her driving around town
with that Larry in his shining roaring car, and figure they could
tell right away what kind of girl the Aldred one was and what she
was in for, too. She, Ellie, had seen them herself in other cars
driven too fast by other wet-lipped, serious boys, had thought
the same thing of other folks' kids. But how (bearing down on
the Sunbeam more than she actually has to, sudden force across
the dress's waist) could it happen and what could you do about
it if Bev truly was going bad? It wasn't that she didn't know the
right things to do. They'd made sure of that, she and Carl, that
neither of the kids would have to do much more after a certain
age than just watch to get it right. And why not? That's how she
and Carl had learned to act, why even when they were young
and going together, they had had their good times (whirling at

the dances, those square dances, in the patterns they moved and formed, so precise, clapping, brighteyed, seeing Carl skip over and feeling him more inside like she *was* him for a second)—why there hadn't ever been any question of either of them, Carl or her, having to calm down, or keep something straight. So why then with Bev (who she sees, knows, this instant up in the bathroom plastering her eyes and cheeks with gookum and hair with spray), whose fault would it be if something happened to her but her own?

Nobody's. Plain enough. Yet (holding the dress before her, watching it fall right and the light cling at the back of it, dimly, in the fibers), Poor Bev, she thinks right out of nowhere, remembering certain barely memorable lights seen lately in her daughter's eyes. Looking for love, she thinks. And sorts through the basket for Carl's shirt, and puts it on the board, flicking her head once quickly up to glance at the screen (Honey, Desi calls to his wife Lucy, You never going to believe . . .), still perplexed. There were girls in her day too like what Bev threatens to turn into. But back then kids didn't go up on a hill in a car and put an end to themselves when they were hardly old enough to drive; back then, little boys like her Danny scared to death over something would generally, as far as she knew, tell their mothers what it was. (That teacher Mrs. Lang calling the other night. I believe your son has had a terrible fright, Mrs. Aldred. Do you know what it could have been?

I was hoping you might be able to tell *me*.

Nothing you know of has happened at your house, then? the teacher said. I mean, Mrs. Aldred—your husband does drive the ambulance for the funeral parlor sometimes, doesn't he?

Danny doesn't get to know anything more than he has to about that. And what he does, he's known a long time now.

Well, the teacher said. Well, I don't know what it could be then. You've noticed it yourself though?

Keeping her mouth shut a second, running a forefinger up the center of her forehead: Yes.

My only guess left then, this teacher said. And it is just a guess—is that maybe somebody's told him about—well about nuclear war.

What?

The atom bomb. Nuclear war. You know. If somebody told him we have the ability to destroy the world, you know, Mrs.

Aldred. If somebody put it to him like that . . .) Scraping grating
sound of gravel in the driveway getting crushed under the tires
of a car going too fast. She moves quickly across the lights of the
room, into the hall where the front door and the stairs are.
Larry's here, better get a move on, she calls, sour-voiced; then,
turning, takes in the school pictures of Bev and Danny hanging
on the wall beside the coat closet: Bev with her eyes lifted in a
silly look of praying or being in some holy light, Danny grin-
ning a way he doesn't any more. (All I know, Mrs. Lang this
teacher said, is when the fire siren blows when he's in school, he
either gets sick or faints. But he says he's not scared of fires. I
think he's got the idea from somewhere it might be an air-raid.

A what? Carl said later when she told him. Well, he said, let's
ask him.

But when you asked him he just cried; so were you right or
wrong?) Opening the door and finding Larry there, even
though she knows it's him all along, makes her mad; it means
her having to stop thinking about the things that matter, and
turn the light in the hall on herself and let him in. Come on in,
she practically mutters at him, and just about sniffs at the way his
right hand comes up to the side of his forehead and smooths his
hair that's too long and greasy blond caked down. But before
stepping out of the hall, with the front door open, she can look
across the road to where Carl, her husband, coming up from the
garage, has just stepped from the night smack into the circle of a
streetlight. Poor man, she thinks, sadly smiling, heading natu-
rally back to the ironing board in the safe, dimmer corner of the
room, He must be so worn out from today . . .

And what'd be the thing to do if you were right? she wonders;
as she picks up Carl's shirt.

*

The shadow of your smile
when you are gone . . .

Is that the way it goes? How does it go? And here she told
herself she'd never forget those words, the first verse anyway.
Bev Aldred checks for them, to find where they're hiding in her
head, like checking over her face with her eyes in the mirror,
light quick looks and touches sweeping both. By the time she
has found a sore hard spot, one that'll be out for everyone to see
in two, three days (Dammit, she says, pushing on it with a fin-
ger), she has left the song behind and gone back to the movie

itself. The names don't matter, movie names that is. Richard Burton is this minister, and married on top of that to a woman who's pretty enough, maybe, but in a funless skinnyfaced sort of way (grimacing at the long jaw she sees in the mirror, rubbing some Cover Girl on). A blonde. Anyway, he falls in love with Liz Taylor who he's married to in real life, who in this movie has her name, the one she, Bev, can't remember, linked up with a lot of people who are wild and paint and play drum music on the beaches at night, so whose reputation is not good.

Leaning in to the mirror, two inches, maybe less, from the brown mirror eyes staring back at her concentrated too hard for feeling. Let that Maybelline pencil slip or jag off one time and it's all over, all you've got is some crazy line streaking across your face which is, in a very small way, more than just troublesome because you've got to patch it up again. It's almost scary, just a little, when things like that happen. For just a second, anyway, it makes you wonder about your control. But only for a second. And not even then if you keep your mind on it in the first place and do it right.

Anyway, Richard Burton (who even has a couple of kids in this, doesn't he? God, Richard Burton for a father, imagine) and Liz Taylor fall in love with each other very hard and land in very deep water as soon as they do. Because even aside from getting around being a minister with a wife like that, the thing you realize is he's got to figure out if it's okay to be out there dancing in the warm, almost hot rich red orange of those fires on the beach next to the Pacific Ocean, with that light on their faces and swerving smiling curving shadows in the darker place behind them, and a huge oily black man beating out rhythms she could hardly, hardly follow on those drums. (She had her eyes shut. Do you love me?

Yes, this boy Larry said; almost too low to hear. What he is doing hurts. Her skull rests against the door handle.

Really?

Oh yes. Yes, I really do, this boys says, this man, the way he has the unbottoned blouse pulled down below her shoulders, she can hardly get her arms up around him at all.

I love you too. *We are in love and will be very happy always together very young and beautiful.*

And give in to this and, glowing inside, float on this water, down its course, it will hold me and carry,

like a small boat, me with that warmth I can feel, that fire warmth
asking for nuture, inside me, asking to spread.

                                        A silvertipped fish with
an orange flame inside, swimming smoothly

                                        sinking

                                        crackling to a
blaze.

The light of the second feature coming in through the wind-
shield, dull fearful cold pale yellow on his sweaty back. Do you
really love me?)

   Or was that beater a blonde-haired boy? Forgetting all that
just since last night makes her frown at the mirror face, taking
the rollers out of the set brown hair, teasing some of it just a little
in the back.

                    The shadow of your smile
                    when you are done . . .

All of a sudden she remembers: Steve Ketchum, they found him
today! What a tragedy! She remembers his face, sees it for a
second while looking at her mirror face, watching what it's do-
ing. He was in her homeroom, too, in ninth grade. Just last year!
What a tragedy. (Oh hon, Larry says. His voice thick, like com-
ing from underwater, like through lips smeared with mud. She
looks at the glove compartment.

   We'd better stop.

   He pushes himself hard against her down there, groans.

   Come on, Larry

   He will try again tonight.)

   But no, that isn't it. Gone; not done. When you are gone.

   The spraying makes a cloud around the mirror face that
smiles, seeing the face of Richard Burton, face of Liz Taylor, on
the beach with the fires crackling on them. But all that takes
place far away, in California.

                                        *

Is it the streetlight circles, the way they seem more snatching than
entered, pockets that would fix him there if he were not moving so fast;
or the stretches of night between them, almost black now, longer now
he's almost to the house on the edge of town where he lives and his
mother and father and sister live, those gaps, those lightless spaces,
holes, he's got to streak through? Or both together: those grabbing
light instants, the drops into the dark?
   He can see, when he looks at the edge of the hills and, beyond, the

sky filling with stars, no moon but the Light itself which grows and fills the sky, its killing gorgeous blossom unrolling, unfolding into orange, yellow, white, flashing blind in which they all, his mother, father, sister, him, house, road, world and act and motion catch, flare and blaze forever, forever in that unspeakable shine.

And it's this that drives him on as fast as his legs can pedal. But whether he moves toward home, or toward the Light he sees, knows is there, cannot not know; or whether all he sees the Light consume is ravaged, or transfigured into flame; or whether it's the Light of the Bomb that can devour the world and kill everything; or whether, seeing it, he is caught in fear or fury or a sweet shining joy: you couldn't say. He pedals, though, for all he's worth, that's sure; of that, at least, there can be no doubt at all.

Skeeter's Last Reflections

Baptized name, William; but in the main, except when he was in the service, he can't remember being called anything but Skeeter, no more than he can place when he started drinking so hard. Sometimes, though, this comes back to him: a summer night when he was maybe three or four, fishing for river bass with Lij, a hot steamy night with fireflies. And Lij is in a laughing, crazy mood but is calling him Skeeter, which makes him feel good. Or maybe it just makes him feel that way when he thinks back on it now. And wasn't there a kerosene lamp, lit and set up on the bank beneath a tree?

Lij was always around then, laughing at some joke you never could get, drunk, spitting snuff out wherever he pleased and handing out work.

"You boy . . . wheel with the red rim on it, you know that old wagon wheel a few steps out past the barn on the back side. This man here" – pointing at the guy, laughing, showing brown teeth and gums, smelling sour – "says he might want to buy it, so roll it down here . . ."

So off Skeeter would go past the unused empty barn and sheds and coops, past the darkness inside their doors where birds fluttered and cried in the evenings, to the junkpile with no real hope of finding what was wanted there. He would run through it for a while, tromping around back there trying to look careful but looking too fast so the black, green, white, green, black of the junkers and the garbage started to whirl. Then he would trip, probably, fall, maybe cut himself on some jagged pieced of metal. And there he'd sit. Lij would come soon and find it and find him, too, and beat on him a little.

"Use your eyes, boy, your eyes, your eyes, you little turd, you jackass" . . . laughing . . .

Hotter than hell back there, the heat waving off what metal's still unrusted, or cold enough to freeze you dead, junk you stone cold as one of the wrecks, still Lij pushed the waves back, beat out the cold, found what he wanted. Found you too.

"What makes you so dumb boy, so goddamn dumb. Hey?"

His brother would say it too, Zack and Paul, both of them. But it wasn't so bad when they said it. It didn't mean they were going to lick you in that barn, in the dark that smelled of piss or old wet green straw.

Elijah
Elijah
Oh lord he's coming after me

In London, in some bar, with a girl. They had a piano in there, and some nigger was playing it. Sometime just after they shot Paul in Italy, or after the air raids anyway at night, with those giant fires cracking the sky open when you came out on the all clear again. Somewhere in there this nigger is pounding it out over and over, drunk as a dog, eyes rolled back in his head.

"That's my old man's name."

"What, dearie?" she said. You could see the makeup on her without looking very hard, and the pits in her face.

"My old man's name. Elijah. In that song over there the nigger has."

"Oh. Elijah? Isn't that a sweet name now?"

"Yeah, that's my old man's name. They call him Lij."

And Skeeter is his. If they call you anything else, you know who they are. If they call you Willy, Billy, Bill, they do not know you. Starting with teachers, all the way back at school, running through the service and the bosses at the plant. "How's it going today, Bill?" Maybe once a month some one of them would be by from the front offices. In a white shirt, with a tie. Mr. Nevill, Mr. Affleby, Mr. Castino. Would stand beside the roofboard machine he fed, smile, and say "How's it going?"

Laughing . . . "Couldn't be better" . . . hands shaking, sweat popping out beneath his eyes on the heavy fat folds of skin. Laughing . . .

Leave me alone you bastards.

"Willy, one at eight o'clock, coming in low." Swivel in the

turret. The other plane lit by its fire. Sweaty hands on the gun in the tiny space shaken by the shooting. The other plane explodes; the men in the other plane die. Willy shoots the plane down. The girl in the bar, her name was Donna; he was Willy to her, too. Willy, not Skeeter, the whole time he was over there.

Bunch of fucking Nazis, you get to thinking after you've shot so many of them down. I got you, you bastards, I nailed your ass . . .

Every so often, she got them up, all three of them, made them scrub up and put on clean clothes, woolen pants that scratched up the inside of your legs. She wore a black hat with a bunch of cherries on it, dark red and hard to the touch. In church they had to be quiet. People stood to sing, sat to listen, lowered their heads. She did it along with them; her mouth moved, noiselessly. He would lean his head on her arms, sniff the rich brown smell under the perfume.

Sometimes, she would cry. Once she was crying on some piecrust she was rolling out in the kitchen. Where the tears hit, there are round marks on the dough.

"Cmon cmon, for Christ's sake," Lij says. "What the hell's the matter now? Still alive, ain't we" – laughing, rolling his eyes backward. Scraping noise of his hand over the whiskers on his chin. Like the sound of something ripped off something else a long ways away.

Poor old Ma, crying in the pie dough. Salt in the pie.

"How'd you rip them pants," she says. And has a hold of him by the shoulders, her finger bones against his shoulder blades. Maybe she'll hit you in a minute, even though her voice does sound as though she's just running down.

"I don't know."

"Skeeter, I want you to tell me now," Ma says. Her nose is a big long bone, white at the edges, quivering a little.

All three of them got in the dark green car that's all smashed up in back: himself, and Zack, who's still alive and works in shipping at the plant and lives in town, and Paul who dies in Italy. The middle of the front seat is torn, and the stuffing that pokes out around the springs is stained rusty in places. "Look at that, boy," says Zack. "Yeah," Paul says, "somebody got hurt bad." "That's blood," you say. "I drive first," Paul says. "The hell you do," Zack says. "No me!" you say. Everybody grabs onto the wheel.

Zack and Paul have had their fill and gotten out. You are alone in the front seat, staring out through the cracks in the windshield and twisting the wheel from side to side. You are driving over the heaps of cans and garbage out in front of you, right over the little orange fires Lij sets to burn them down for more room, but swerving for the rest of the wrecks, for they are moving too. The garbage dumps flatten out and are a road; you are alone, driving at night . . .

Ma is dead, and Lij is dead, and Paul is dead, and the people in the other planes are dead.

"Sure used to cry a lot, didn't she?"

"Oh yeah; yes she did." Lij shades his head, smiles. Most of his teeth are gone. The ones left give him enough trouble that he complains of them every so often. Sitting at the table, washing down the last of supper, cans of hash and some corn Orton Skelley down the way gave them, with a cold one. The radio on, the news from Korea coming out. Lij laughs a little, picks up his can of Genessee. His eyes roll back as he drinks.

"What you laughing at now?"

"Oh, just them chinks. Boy, you got to hand it to them. Fuckers just come and come."

Later, maybe that same night, putting the dishes in the sink to do tomorrow. "Had a lot of aches and pains, she did, "Lij says from over at the table still. Right out of nowhere he says it, looking off towards the wall with that crazy smile on his face. Just looking at the wall.

And for just a second it feels like it'd be worth killing the bastard just to wipe that smile off his fucking face. Then, just as quick, like it's not a smile at all: like all these years that crazy look has never been what you could rightly call a smile after all.

"Is that so? Nobody ever told me."

"Well she had them all right, " Lij says. "She just never could quite get used to things." And the crazy look that's not a smile deepens on his face.

Out the window above the sink, the shadows from the back hill have already spilled over the hayfield on the side hill and eaten up half the junk piles. And the sun coming straight through the window at him makes it look like the junk just stops at the edge of the light, and from there all the way to the top of the back hill is pure black, nothing.

When he turned around again, Lij had gone under. But his

lowered head still dangled just off the table. He got him up and on the bed upstairs and went on down the road to Tommy's Bar to get a few more in himself.

In the summertime in Tommy's or at the Club, they always have an old joke about him. Whoever's there, Chekkie Otway or Jackie Kerian or whoever, they always have it ready for him. "Skeeter, how many bales you get in tonight?" they say.

"Oh, three, four hundred."

Then sometimes they say "What is it now, Skeeter? You're already on second cut now, huh?"

"Hell yes, first cut's been in the barn now for two months."

"Good hay?" they say.

"You bet your fucking life, jack."

Everybody around gets a good laugh out of that one. Who knows, for Chrissake, the last time that sonofabitchin field was cut and baled? So long ago there wouldn't be anything really up there on the side hill any more but a bunch of fucking ragweed and thorns. Sometime back before Lij was even dead.

Or after work, when everybody is sitting lined up against the yellow walls of plant one waiting to be let out through the gate, elbows on their knees, swinging lunch pails between their legs, whistling, shredding grass with their fingers and throwing it on the sidewalk, watching the cars go out on the road: then too, lots of times somebody'll say "How many bales you expect to get in tonight Skeeter?" And everybody laughs and kills some time that way, too.

You learn to keep yourself busy on a job like that, not like when he and Lij had the garbage business. There you got to see people, plus get in and out of the flatbed truck with the week's trash they threw out. And even some of that was worth a good look; you'd be surprised at the stuff sometimes. Perfectly good stuff, some of it, clothes and food. Once Lij found a bottle of Cutty Sark half full and they were off the rest of the day; went straight up Dexter Hollow and drank it down under the maple trees.

But the sad thing of that job was when you found somebody's snapshots in a can. Some even with frames still on them: people's faces nobody saw again.

This one night, not too long ago, instead of going home from wherever he had been, he drove straight into town and pulled the Buick up at the church. For a few minutes he just turned his head and rested it against the seat. The moon made the white church glow. But over the doorway another roof stuck out that cut out the light and made the whole entrance fuzzy and dark. He started to cry in a couple of minutes, he was that drunk. Couldn't for the life of him have told you why.

You have to keep yourself busy. After you've been doing it, feeding the chunks of foamglass in for five, six years or so, you don't need to have anything on your mind. It's just on breaks, lunchtime, and the ten minute dead time before getting out that you have to think of something to do: hum or whistle or laugh at somebody else's shenanigans; pinches, slaps, sneaking up on somebody else and pretending you're buttfucking them.

Garth, next to him at the bar now, he'll do that. He'll come after you right while you're on the line. Just come up behind you and smack himself against you and groan loud. It's all he thinks about too, working over there on the finish end. You work with a fellow long enough, you go around with him, you get so you know that sort of thing about him; and that is all Garth thinks about, is fucking.

"Hey goddammit cut that out, you," you'll say, turning around so fast you can feel the fat shake in your cheeks; and maybe throw a fist out at him to push him back.

"Well you look like a nice fat old bitch," Garth'll say, and laugh. "You fat old pusgut." Then he'll wipe his black hair off his forehead and the smile will fade.

He'll do it just anywhere, at a bar in front of people, or in the plant, or anywhere.

But he's a good fellow. They're all good fellows. You sit there and have a drink and think about them all, god love them, and it's enough to make you cry. But when you're with them you just laugh and laugh, because they're all such good fellows.

"God love you, Garth," you say out loud, and clink your glass of beer against his.

Garth's mouth tightens and draws downward. He shoots you a hard look, a hot red face, bushy eyebrows. "Yeah, you old sonofabitch, sure," he says and looks down the bar away from you again. Looking for somebody to fuck. And you look back down at your beer.

Heaps of cans and paper and dirt, garbage flicked with fire, settling slowly down against the ground. Sometimes from up there in the plane that's what those cities looked like. Junked cars rearing up all around them, flak exploding in the air. He would press on the pedal and the turret would turn, humming in his ears, going around and around and around.

Bright sweet blond hair, big tits, pink birthmark on her neck: Betsy Dorty. Paul got to her first, and died in Italy. They never said how. Boy, skinny Paul with his thick lips, his crazy dark brown eyes.

What a heller he was! Drink all night, that boy. Fight at the drop of a hat. More ass than you could shake a stick at. Yes, more than just Betsy. There he was this one morning, out squatted on that pile nearest the barn, buck naked, bruises on his face you could see from your bedroom, crying out: Cock-a-doodle-do! And flapping his arms like wings. You could hear him from the bedroom, see his breath steam in the fall morning air, and the leaves on the trees on the hills beyond on fire with reds, oranges, browns . . .

"She just never could quite get used to it," Lij told him. And here he'd never even known she hurt.

There was that Donna girl when he was in London, her and a couple of others. You got drunk enough so things would start to turn fast enough, like a sad song speeded up to happy. Then you end up pumping in and out of them all right, but that's not the point. You're just doing that because you're there, really: you've gotten where you can see you're still alive and kicking, so you kick. Then the next morning, their hair is in your face, the smell of what you did sits in the room like dead flat beer, you feel like something thrown away, thrown out: twisted, wrecked, empty. So it's time to start over again. Fingers twitch for your pants, you count the change . . .

Got out after a minute or two when he had had enough of snuffling in the car. It was snowing out, light and brittle snow like pellets, he'd left his jacket behind someplace. Cold enough so he was shivering by the time he got inside. The place was all lit up, and warm. Sweet smell of perfume in the air, and six or seven women running around up by the altar who all turn around and stop dead when he walks in.

˙ "Can I help you?" one of them says.

Oh he knew them, most of them anyway. Couldn't think of their names but he knew them all right. Went to school with some of them, known of who they married, picked out snap-shots from their trash.

"Are you sure you're in the right place?"

"Going to church," he says.

One of them laughs. Two others come down off the raised-up section where the priest and choir are and all, and walk back towards him. He lowers down in a pew.

"There's no church now," one of the two says. "We're just setting up the altar."

He raises his hand, waves it at them, shakes his head. "This's a church. Leave me alone. This's a goddamn church."

"Now now now," this grey-haired woman says. What the hell was her name anyway? Has her hand out like she's going to touch him but just decided not to. "Wouldn't you rather come back when you're feeling a little better?"

He would look up at her face crowned in that black circle of hat. The cherries dripped over the side. You could see right up into her nose. You could feel her breath through the thin cotton of her dress. Feel her bones. Smell the skin stretched over the bones. The smell, warm and rich, floats in your head . . . lingers there . . . you are alive.

Sometimes he says to himself By god I will do some haying tonight. Go down to Orton Skelly's and borrow his rig and get up on that side hill and do it. Half-thinks it anyway, like those pictures that come at you so fast when you're just finally waking up in the morning. Rats from the junk piles are in the house, too. Upstairs in the bedroom Lij and Ma had the windows are all knocked out by some smartass kids. The other night, how long ago was that now? – the goddamn porch, a couple boards gave out and there he fell, down through under there in the cold musty dark, lying on his side in the dark, drunk beneath the house. Everything come to a dead stop.

"Belong here," you say. All you'd really like to do by this time is lay your head down on the pew. You can feel how fat your face is, how heavy the flesh on your face. The women should go away. "Used to come here, this church, all the time," you say.

But no, the women shake their heads at you, and things have slowed down too much. No smells either, except for the beer on your breath. You're just drunk in another place where they don't want you, don't know you, and it's time to go home.

"Night, ladies, g'night" . . . laughing . . . "sorry to bother" . . . back to the snow and the car and the trip home, laughing all the way.

Sweet ladies.

Betsy Dorty up against the barn wall. Still smelling of rot and birdshit in there, and Paul away for the war, still stationed down in Fort Bragg at the time. She wants it bad, jesus but she does. High up the inside of her legs wet to the touch, that's how bad. "Aw cmon cmon cmon" she keeps saying to him til he hardly has a chance to get his own pants any lower than his knees. And there, with Paul gone, and Lij off somewhere drunk and Ma in the kitchen, he gives it to this girl in the dark of the barn, hearing the birds flutter, fly from the beams. But it isn't right. He shakes the whole time at the wrong he does. Oh the sky busts open and she pulls you to her and all that, but she is your brother's girl, your brother's baby and don't you forget it, for he will die, dies in Italy. Outside are the junked cars and the garbage. She moans at the wrong speed.

Do it at the right speed, it doesn't fuck you up. You keep your job and don't have time to stand around.

Otherwise, you take Garth now. Best friend he has in the damn world and there he sits always looking like he's about to kill the next person to say Boo. Gets into it wherever they go. Talking about fucking all the time, scratching at himself. Spends every free minute he has thinking one thing or another: fighting or fucking. Stands over there on the other side of the machine throwing the roof-board sheets off as fast as he can, til by the end of a day when they get to Tommy's or the Club or someplace out of town altogether, he's about ready to kill.

Take a few minutes ago, just after they first got here: Garth says, "How many times you ever fuck in a night?"

"Oh plenty, jack, plenty." All the time looking at that mirror along the bar, past the colored brown, red, green, white of all the bottles.

"Night I was married, it was eleven times, eleven goddamn times," Garth says.

Just smiling . . . looking at those bottles . . .

"Hey what the fuck's so funny about that your goddamn chickenshit bastard," Garth says, and pushes against your shoulder. Done it once, he's done it a hundred times. You have to smile and laugh again, and smack him on the back, and say something.

"My name's Robert R. but everybody calls me Raggedy-Ass Bill," you say, anything like that, anything at all. Then he sees you're drunk and lets up a little. But the poor sonofabitch never has a good time.

There he is right now, mouthing off down the bar with some guy he's never seen before in his life, nine chances out of ten. "Meat loaf?" Garth says, real loud, staring around as if he's looking for something to tear off the walls. "Are you shitting me? Shit, hamburg's fucked up enough as it is. Goddamn meat loaf's just adding insult to injury."

The other fellow says something you can't hear. A few people look up from the pool table.

"Yeah, you shit too," Garth says, practically yelling. "Let your own goddamn meat loaf. I bet you do."

And here they drove straight from work an hour to get to this place because Garth wanted to come. He was always like that. Want to go to some new place, he'd say, meet some new blood, maybe find a little snatch. Then get into some kind of fight as soon as he walked in the door. Poor old sonofabitch, can't even tell a joke right. Like just now, with that meat loaf. Now that could've been a good one, could've meant nothing serious at all. But that was the way with Garth about jokes. He was the same with the haying one. You just had to leave him alone.

"Use your eyes, boy, your eyes, your eyes," Lij said, laughing . . .

Turn your eyes away from him to the hard shiny wood under your head at the bar. Wherever the hell he is, they have the good music here, the old stuff with the sweet women's voices in front, violins going to town in the back. Sentimental journey . . . love's old sweet song . . .

Elijah
Ooooh Elijah
Lord he's coming after me

"What is it deary?" this woman, this Donna asked with the fires eating up the night outside. But this music is not like that nigger banging away at that piano in that bar in London. Not a bit. This is smoother, and it moves just right.

Lij was still lying there in bed when he went in. A half full can of beer on the floor beside the bed, and his mouth curled up in the laugh, like he had almost been ready to do it one more time.

Poor old Ma, dying for somewhere around a year, back around '46, '47. Wouldn't go to a hospital, just laid there til her face was a skill and the house smelled of the cancer anywhere you were in it: sweet, heavy stink. Then she died.

But Paul dies in Italy; who knows about Paul? It's hard without a picture of Paul, some quiet soundless picture like on the tv up above this bar when all you can hear is that sweet lady, easy violins; that sentimental journey. Here on tv somebody gets shot or walks up with a can of something and smiles, but the music from the jukebox always drowns it out. But without a picture of Paul? Of Paul in Italy?

Shit, as far as that goes, where's a picture for Betsy Dorty being married now with kids and living down along the River Road someplace, after leaning up against that barn and saying Cmon cmon cmon? For Zack living in town now in a house on the main drag down from the plant where he's a goddamn foreman, hardly speaks to you now? Aluminum siding just put up on his house, wife and two, three kids? Where's the way all that looks and moves? When you come right down to it, it's as hard as Paul dead in Italy.

Lying there doubled up in the dark, dead drunk. Looking up, the smallest chink of sky through the hole in the boards. Still, those stars, white and still and clean. But the rats are running around down there, down where you are . . .

Was there a fight? Garth is dragging some girl up from her seat, trying to get her to dance.

Underneath, the clean square cities, those buildings blowing up in lines. Tracers spit into the night like orange, white arrows. It does no damn good to fire at them either. If they are going to hit, if the flak is going to crash through the turret, there's not a damn thing you can do to stop it.

Leave me alone you bastards.

Those beer sweats start coming out some mornings about nine. Hands start to shake and fumble, sometimes crack one or two of the foamglass squares. Those white shirts from the front office might be out there, might come out any time. Or the belt gets ahead, and you have to dump them on for all you're worth for a while, speed up because things are moving too goddamn slow. They're all but stopped. Some picture is stuck in your head: a hat with cherries on it, a smile of brown, crooked teeth, fires in the night. And you have to get things moving again.

Like tonight on the way up, turning to look at Garth's face lit yellow by the dash lights, frowning, staring out through the windshield into the night; and wondering all of a sudden What the hell is this anyway? What the hell's going on? Who is this face, this other fellow in the car?

Think that way long enough and it'll get to you; but nobody means anything by it. They're all good old fellows. Stop and think about it and you're dead, the foamglass cracks, you end up in a goddamn church where nobody even knows your fucking name.

Now it's all all right, though, when it's like this, however the hell you got out here. Out here in the parking lot with all these cars with the red neon of the beer sign warming, licking at their metal and glass. Just standing out here waiting for Garth to finish off whatever the hell he's into, why everything's just fine. The pictures blur and slide by, you can even close your eyes and the pictures will float by as you walk. Had just enough to drink so that the whole black night beyond you turns around and around at just the right speed, fills with whatever pictures you put in it, fading into the night around you just fast enough as you walk along past the cars, moving at just the right speed, you Skeeter, you, alive and kicking. All the pictures come together, dance around you in the night, you standing in the road. Then, at just the right speed, blur and blend into the two white lights, the growing noise in the background . . .

He turns to watch the lights; and is still smiling, standing quite still, when the car hits; and all the pictures glow one more instant, very bright.

The Night Game

The night Susie came to feel slapped in the face, the basket-ball game was away. So the seven of them, herself and Mel and their whole old circle of friends had gathered at the Lewises to drink some drinks and eat some snacks and to root for the Beavers on tv. Towards the end of the game, things got pretty close, Armstrong fouled out early thanks to some calls the men agreed were pretty shady, and they let things slide so much in the last few minutes that it finally brought Carl in his orange and black sweater up off the rocking chair, jumping up and down yelling "Defense! Defense!" at the little figures running around on the set.

And of course at that point Carl's wife Nancy couldn't resist one of her dry jokes – "Sit down, Carl," she said from her perch on the couch beside Susie, "you're off your rocker, sit down" – or maybe something else, but that was the gist of it anyway.

And they all laughed – Susie's own husband Mel, leaning against the wall nearest the table with all the food, Dick and Ann Lewis in the matched plaid armchairs across the room, and Frank Bjornlund laughing, big deep chuffs of laughter coming out of his large, square, bearded face. Just a little thing really, but it would come back to her afterwards: how Frank Bjornlund had laughed too, how she had noticed it.

In the end, of course, the Beavers pulled it out as they had all season now up through the playoffs, one great game after the other. Then, right at the start of the post-game show when Coach Miller had just stepped up to the mike looking grim but happy and they were just starting to settle down from all the jumping up and clapping and hugging their husbands and wives, Mel's beeper went off in his pocket and he had to take his arm

out from around Susie's waist, put his sandwich down and an-
swer it. He was on call that night at the hospital and wouldn't
you know, something had come up; someone was hemorrhag-
ing or something and he had to get right up there. They all
groaned when Mel told them, pulling his coat on on his way out
the door, wrapping the cashmere scarf she had put in his stock-
ing for Christmas that year around his throat; but they were all
used to it, really, Dick was a doctor too up at the hospital, and
even Carl as a lawyer got his share of emergency calls. Only
Frank as a professor had no such problems; so over the years
they had learned to groan and laugh it off. Susie, as usual, would
stay behind, finish the party out, get a ride home with one of the
others amid whose fond cries of farewell Mel stepped out the
door, into the BMW, and drove away.

Only later, when she looked back on it, when the whole night
had gone strange and she was thinking of answers to things she
could not remember asking, questions floating up from her own
mind – only then did she think back and wonder how and why
it had seemed so obvious to everyone, including her, that Frank
should be the one to take her home. An hour or so went by
while the men listened to the Coach, agreed and disagreed, had
another drink or two, replayed the game, while the women sat
around the couch and traded stories and notes: Nancy's little
Bob was on the junior high soccer team and starting to act his
age around girls, Nancy thought he'd actually be dating soon; in
a month Anne's oldest daughter Brenda would be getting her
driver's permit; Susie talked a while herself about her own
daughter, Marie, and the current struggle over whether or not
she would stop taking flute now that she said she was so tired of
it; and Frank, Frank himself called over once from across the
room where the men were standing, joining in to describe his
own son Marty's new commitment to running, up at 6 every
morning to hit the roads and shower down before school.
Nothing out of the ordinary in all this, of course, everything
easy and taken-for-granted in its way, the way they had evolved
over the years. The whole thing was of course about couples,
families, children, as it had always been, naturally – just as natu-
ral as was the unspoken decision by all concerned that as the two
halves of two incomplete couples Frank and Susie provisionally
fit. Carl and Nancy would go back by themselves, alone.
Though their house too was up in the hills, far closer to Susie's

than Frank's (down in town, on the flats) it was Frank who would take her back home.

It was somewhere around midnight when they left Dick and Ann wrapped together on the porch, waving goodnight at the other couples getting into their respective cars, at her getting in with Frank without a second thought. The car was his old red Toyota; as they sat and listened to the motor cranking, puttering up, Susie noticed snowlike dust on the dashboard, the ground-in smell of his pipesmoke hanging stale in the closed car, and for some reason thought of Aileen. Was she really his ex-wife now, was the divorce legally through? Susie was all set to ask but then didn't: it had been, after all, just a nice light evening and Frank was always so serious anyway, it was an old joke among them, how serious he always looked, at least. Plus when you came right down to it she knew it was none of her business anyway.

So neither of them had said a word yet to each other when Frank put the car in gear and drove away. She was half expecting it to be like that the whole way home, even enjoying it – after all the talks and drinks and laughter, the excitement of the game, just letting yourself sink back and watch the streets and houses slide by without bothering to think where they were, where you were, who you were with or what you ought to say next, know-ing Frank wouldn't mind if you did. She was thinking or half-thinking something about whether or not to get up for church tomorrow, though the fact of the matter was, she and Mel had stopped years ago. After nights out like this, though, that was the point; it was just something to roll over when you weren't really thinking of anything at all, when there was nothing you really had to say.

And then he spoke.

"I'm not going to do this any more," Frank Bjornlund said. "I'm shit-sick of this stuff."

At first Susie thought it was a joke she hadn't gotten; "shit-sick" was new to her and sounded funny, she was smiling, al-most laughing when she turned to look at him. Then by the time she could tell from his face he wasn't kidding, the words were already chuckling out of her mouth, she had already answered:

"What stuff?"

Frank didn't look back. In fact it was as though she weren't even there, he was all alone and his long face with its neat clipped fringe of beard spoke just to itself, staring out at the shiny wet blacktop.

"Should have called her up, not me," he was saying. "She's the one who always liked it."

Susie gathered he meant Aileen. She was starting to catch on to the rest of it too. Under her car coat her upper arms felt cold. She rubbed them with her hands to keep from shivering all over. She knew why they had never called Aileen for anything from the time when Aileen left last year to now, but it seemed so obvious it was hard to put into words. Instead of answering, she looked out the window, really looking this time. They were off the flats, the houses were getting bigger, they were moving uphill on Grant towards Timberline, her neighborhood, where her house and family were. It wouldn't be long now in any case.

Frank turned right onto the street cutting across the hillside, her street. He was driving slowly, cautiously, still with that same quiet look. It was only a matter of a few blocks. "You know what, Susie?" he said.

She had a terrible feeling about what was coming, whatever it would be. The awful thing about it was you had to answer, you were trapped. "What?" she heard herself say in a dark quiet voice like his.

"I know that you and Mel are not bad people." Frank said, still looking straight forward steadily, as if examining the windshield for cracks. "But I don't like you. Not just you two, the whole bunch of us – including me by now, I guess." He made his little laughing sound deep in his throat which she had heard of course a million times before at various dinners, parties, gettogethers through the years, a dry academic laughter which seemed very scary now.

"Sometimes when I'm with you, when we're all together like just now, I think I'm going straight out of my mind," said Frank.

Later she would have time to go back over everything that rushed into her head, all the things she could have said and almost did. Oh Frank, she could have said, you're just upset, and then gone on to ask him in for coffee or a drink and find out more, with Mel there too maybe, about whatever was really on his mind, the divorce itself or what. She could have gotten mad and told him off, called him a snob or something on the order of that. She could have even asked him why – why didn't he like her, or Mel, or the rest of them? Why not, after all these years of at least pretending to? But at the time all this just smeared by, followed by all she could think of next, which was how much she just wanted to get out of here, this dingy little car she was stuck in with him. She looked up again; there was their house coming up with the porch light on over the oak door, kitchen light inside glowing the curtains soft over the sink, saying Forget this conversation, it never happened, in another minute you'll be in here with us. The BMW was in the drive too, so Mel was home. Frank pulled up behind it and shut the motor off. The silence following was unbelievably terrible. She was looking at her hands folded up in her lap.

"I doubt you'll tell anybody what I've just told you," Frank said. One of his hands, his left hand was fumbling for something in his coat, she could see it out of the corner of her eye, like one of those nightmares where you cannot speak or move to stop what they are going to do to you, when all you can do is just watch. He hauled out his pipe, pipe tool and tobacco pouch, put them up on the dash, started pinching tobacco from the pouch into the pipe. He was still looking straight ahead, off in his thoughts. "Good night, Susie," he said.

Then she could leave.

She heard his car start up when she was hanging up her coat in the front closet. Whether that meant he had watched her in or not, she didn't know, would never know. It seemed just as likely he had spent the time puffing his pipe and staring straight out at the back of Mel's car, the garage, the house, as if the whole hillside of homes and streets were no more than some giant dark space he stood on the edge of, looking down and in.

*

On her way down the hallway she looked in to make sure Marie was back from the movies and in bed: sure enough. When she walked out of the bathroom after washing off her makeup, there was Mel in their own bed, awake but only just, with his head still propped on the pillows but the *Newsweek* lying face down at his side. One look at him and any idea she might have had of telling him what had just happened flew right out of her head.

"Good time?" Mel said thickly.

"Oh sure," she said in a quick light voice that might have made him sit up and take notice, ask her what was the matter had he not been so far gone. Susie took her outfit off – the grey ruffled blouse, the tartan skirt, the sort of thing they all said only she looked young enough to get away with – shook it out, hung it up, tossed her underthings in the hamper. Behind her back she heard Mel rolling over, sighing, settling in. When his bedside lamp went out something went off in her.

"Things go all right at the hospital?" she said, loud enough that he would have to answer, no matter how far out he was.

"Hrnn?" came her husband's startled voice. "Hyeh, uh-huh. He'll come around." Followed immediately by his deep regular breaths, diving down to sleep. She could have said, Frank tried to rape me on the way home, he pulled out a gun and tried to kill himself, he broke down and cried on my lap like a kid, and it would have made no difference. Once Mel was gone he was gone.

Her eyes by now were used to the dark. When she slid the clothescloset open she could make out her clothes by their shapes, the way things hung and fell. The nightgown she chose was a light, sunny yellow, though of course you couldn't tell its color now. The reason why they asked Frank to things and not Aileen was, Number One, that Aileen was the one who had left; Number Two, of the two of them Frank was the one who needed the company and support anyway, everyone knew Aileen would do just fine. Which led to Number Three: which was, no matter how much they liked Aileen (a lot, over the years) she *had* left her husband and son after almost twenty years of it and no problems any of the rest of them had known about, to go off and live back on 29th or 30th, one of those streets in the student section with a much, much younger man with whom she was now going back to school herself, in what, computer science? at the very same university where her ex-husband poor Frank taught for crying out loud. Not (of course) that there was *necessarily* anything wrong with any of it, even leaving Frank who god knows couldn't have been the easiest person in the world to live with for a person as outgoing as Aileen, no matter how interesting he really was underneath. But for all these reasons, Numbers One, Two, and Three, it wouldn't have been comfortable, they would always feel funny with her. Supposing she showed up with her boyfriend, for example, how would Carl and Mel and Dick have felt about that? Suppose she sat down with her and Ann and Nancy and told them all what classes she was taking, what her gradepoint was, how well things were going, you know, between her and this young stud she had picked up and who for all they knew might well be living off her (and, indirectly, Frank) as well? It would never have been comfortable, could never have been right.

Well. All right then, She stopped just standing there without a stitch on in the middle of the room, the middle of the night; she slipped the nightgown on, moved for the bed.

And there was no reason to think Aileen minded it either, for that matter. Take the last time they ran into each other, a month or so ago in Zayre's. Aileen must have known the blue tapered candles she was buying would be dinner party candles for a night at her and Mel's, but it didn't seem to faze Aileen a bit. She herself was after some bulbs for those special bright lamps, Tensors – Marie had one in her room, at her desk. In fact, they had a very nice quick little chat together about the kids, Aileen telling her what Marty was up to these days, her filling her in on Marie, right there at the checkstand before hurrying off. It was perfectly obvious Aileen had no hard feelings. As a matter of fact, if the truth be known, she seemed just as glad to get away, to be off the hook at last.

Here, now, it still felt cold, even with the nightgown on. That same chill from the way home wouldn't go away. When she slid in under the covers, Mel was fully in position, on his side, his back to her. His bald spot glowed dully, like a fuzzy white disc. She reached out, rubbed the hot soft back under the pajamas; since putting on weight these past few years, he was always just a furnace, a whole heating system in himself.

They might still talk about it sometime, she supposed. He had, after all, talked as much about Mel as about her, so Mel had a right to know. Not right now, though, of course. No sense getting him all worked up over a few stray remarks, some silly little thoughtless thing like this.

Besides, what made the two of them – yes, Aileen too for that matter, before or after shacking up with her new boy – what made them think they were so special, extra stuff on the stick? Did they really think Carl always got that jumping up-and-down excited and Nancy made her wisecrack afterwards because it just happened, they were like that over and over again because they were just plain dumb? That everybody found the Carl-and-Nancy act a total riot every time, and all the rest of

them always got all choked up at the sight of the Lewises in an-
other set of identical sweaters, smiling their secret smiles at each
other then out at you though they were all by now at least forty-
two, forty-three for crying out loud and had been going around
together almost as long as they'd been married, trying to outrun
the incredible goddamn boredom of living a life in a small quiet
nice town like this without going straight out of your mind? Did
they think she didn't want to gag herself sometimes at the sound
of her own cotton voice talking about Marie and roller skates,
Marie and driver's ed, Marie and the flute, at the sight of Mel
stuffing more food in his face and lifting his fat hands to tell
someone one of his pathetic jokes, the ones he gets from the
other guys up at the clinic who get them from the drug salesmen
who drop off a sample or two of the newest whatever-it-is, slob-
ber out their stupid dirty stories then take off? What gave the
two of them the right to think they were somehow exempt?

It took another minute for Susie to catch herself and realize
how funny she must look sitting up like this with her arms
around her ribs hugging herself like a looney in a straight jacket,
staring off like Frank himself back in the car. No use getting all
wound up just because you can't please everyone. Nothing to
lose sleep over no matter what.

Though of course it was all the more a shame when the peo-
ple who didn't like you turned out to be the people you'd gone
around with for years on the assumption that they did.

But it *wasn't* just an assumption, either. Rather than sliding
down, Susie sat up more instead. She reached behind and
tipped the pillows up against the bronze bedstead, then settled
back as if watching the late show on the Sony on the chest of
drawers by the closet, across from the foot of the bed.

And the funny thing was, it really was like a movie, quick
scenes of Frank and Aileen over the years, from the time when
Carl – it was Carl, wasn't it? – first met Frank when they shared
a court out at the racquet club just after it first opened and first
asked him and his wife Aileen to a post-football-game party,
from that time and that party on. A bright brilliant fall day, one
of those before the leaves have gone, when you feel like they
never will, and the rainy winter is a million years away. Nancy
had outdone herself with a huge batch of Chinese hors
d'oeuvres which had obviously taken hours to make but were
gone in a matter of seconds, they were so good. Back then all the

the women including herself had a least one baby in their arms or another one crawling around, but she could still see Aileen sitting there on the couch with the rest of them, talking and eating a little but mainly just listening and smiling or frowning, saying yes or no, nodding That's great or shaking That's awful to whatever it was they talked about back then – husbands and children probably, same as now. She remembered how it was that afternoon and other afternoons and evenings for a good long time: she remembered Aileen's smooth cheerful face, how grateful it looked, how her eyes followed yours. How even quiet Frank back then before tenure or beard stood talking to Mel, Carl and Dick with exactly the same look on his face. *Let us in. We'll do what you want. We want to be like you.*

And they more or less had. There were shopping trips to Portland Aileen could hardly afford, of course, vacation trips to Japan and the Bermudas, etc., whose lengths of stay and distances she and Frank could not hope to match, but that was okay. They could still be in on these sports parties, dinner parties, get-togethers, weekend camping trips, all the good pleasant times and scenes. They could let them in anyway, they were so nice – the quiet nice professor and his nice quiet wife.

And look what you got for it now: slapped in the face.

Slapped in the face: she repeated the phrase to herself, half aloud. Yet she realized that at some point in the middle of that last whole chain of thoughts, without her noticing it her mood had changed. She felt sad, and sick to her stomach now, like she could even throw up. The fact was, there had been some differences all the way along. The arguments Frank got himself teased into on health insurance by Dick and Mel the doctors of course, with Carl grinning off to the side. Or back during the sixties Aileen's horrible seriousness there for a while, calling up every day practically to say Have you written that letter, made this phone call, would they all be at some march or demonstration none of them would be caught dead at, however much they were all more or less on her side, until you started to think twice about asking them over and possibly having to go through the whole thing again, what a hideous monstrous genocidal thing it was, etc. etc. "How's your work with the hippies going?" Carl or Dick or Mel would say across the table set for dinner or buffet. "Stopped the war yet this week?" Then Frank would blush and look away, Aileen's face would go white, she would start in with that same old stuff again, not knowing they were just having a little fun with her.

But it *was* such a shame: all that time and talk and food and laughter gone down the drain as far as the two of them were concerned. Why in the world had they wanted it so if they hated it this much now? Looking back on those days now, with what Frank had just said on top, Susie saw them all again – still young and happy, with all their differences – and felt like crying. Good friends, good times, tears welling hot and wet. Rather than give in she blinked them back, once twice three times. She leaned forward, peering over Mel to catch the time on the nightstand alarm. No wonder she was tired and sad: 2:45!

She slid back down under the blankets and tried to sleep. She rolled against Mel's hot plush body, pressed the side of her face so firmly against his padded shoulder she could feel his steady heartbeat, breathe with his breath. It had worked often enough before, but not this time. Instead she realized that she really had started to cry.

He was a good, a good man, a good husband, a good father, a great guy but she wished to hell he would wake up and comfort her, tell her there was nothing to it, hug her, tell her Go back to sleep now. It was just as much about him, after all! She was actually sobbing, right out loud. It went on for some time, stopping only when she was completely exhausted – aching, feverish, watery-boned. When she looked up and over again it was five of 3, Jesus Christ. The bedroom was amazingly, totally silent, with a high soundless singing in the air. But her stomach at the same time felt worse and worse. A sour burning bubble rose and broke out of her throat, along her tongue, and once again she was close – even closer now, to gagging. Right on the verge.

And made it to the bathroom just in time, though nothing much came up or out but some hot bitter strings. Afterwards she stayed there quite a while on the cold tiles, with her head hanging over the edge of the bowl, looking down at the slight, rippling patterns of water, thinking nothing, feeling nothing, not even half bad. When she finally got up words had come back, she was thinking things again. But there was still that clarity. She was standing at the white sink, in front of the mirror, watching the face they all said looked so young, like Marie's sister they said, as though she had never grown up. Well, it hardly looked like that now. The only thing that looked even alive was the eyes, and they were the eyes of some kind of dog, what kind, what was she thinking of? "Spaniel," she said out loud, and watched the face, lips, teeth, cheeks crinkle into a quick smile then smooth back the instant she clicked off the bathroom light.

Then she was back in the bedroom again, which seemed now both bigger and emptier. Mel rolled over as she watched; his arm flopped out on her half of the bed, the space where she usually lay; his low groan reached her like a very distant cry. She walked ahead, beyond nightstand and bed, past the chest of drawers and walk-in closet, over the pile carpeting, aware of moving as though she meant every step of the way. The same with drawing the cord that gathered the drapes away from the bedroom's picture window, so as to stare out past the shrubs, over the lawn and road and houses across the way, out past them and down to the lights lining the streets in town, dotting the little houses here and there.

Something had happened; all her sorrow, anger, fatigue were gone; she had come to realize, way down deep, that she knew Frank and Aileen were right. Together with Mel, and Nancy and Carl, and Ann and Dick, she hadn't paid attention, hadn't thought about enough. Not that she was all that sure what she was thinking now, but it was a lot anyway. Something like that all those people down there were alive, on this world, just like here with their husbands and wives and kids and houses and all that stuff, and she never really acted like they were. So was Mel, for that matter. So was Marie. She knew that more and better about them of course, Mel and Marie, she loved them after all, took care of them and talked about them all the time to Nancy and Ann and all her other friends, but still. That was what Frank was talking about, wasn't it? That was why Frank and Aileen hated them so much.

The bright patterning lights of the streets and houses out beneath, beyond her own sparkled back at her as though from some great clear place on the other side of the hazy winter rain still falling on her street, her neighborhood, her lawn up here. She looked down on them for a long, indeterminably long time, holding the edge of the curtains aside with one gently raised hand, around her hearing the heated air breathed through the bedroom vents. She was different already, she had already changed. She would be sensitive from now on, pay attention to people, take things seriously. She would be alive. She could feel it in her chest, her heart, like great sorrow or joy. Her feet had grown so cold that they were numb, her legs and arms had goosebumps; still she stayed there looking down for a long, caring, wonderful time.

Then, even when she did finally get into bed – at 4:08, she sneaked a look – she still could not fall asleep right away, tired and happy though she was. Behind her closed eyes she saw the three of them – no Mel, no Marie. They were sitting at a plain wooden kitchen table painted white, like the one she imagined where Aileen lived now, in her apartment or whatever in the student part of town. But without the student there (whoever he was), just her and Frank and Aileen with their elbows on the table, talking of serious, substantial things, things that mattered – life and death, politics – lifting smoking white mugs to their lips between thoughts, between words. They were walking, all three of them, along some kind of flatland, maybe a beach but not so pretty though the sunset off in the distance was really quite nice. They were still talking, still about the same real and important things, and it seemed they were moving steadily, getting somewhere too in spite of the hard wind trembling Frank's beard streaming Aileen's long hair streaked with grey waking up lighting up her own cheeks her whole face blowing their words out of reach.

And she did not know that nothing would happen, nothing would change, this was as close to it as she could get. That thanks to Marie's special weekend swim team practice for the upcoming regionals she would have to get up in just five hours to fix their Sunday breakfast, waffles and sausage, early enough that they could all sit down and eat together without Marie getting all upset over how much she had to digest before practice, assuming she would eat at all. That afterwards, when she and Mel were together alone on the couch across from the front room fireplace, looking through the Sunday paper while Mel waited for the ball games to start, she would think only once of saying anything about this last night, either what Frank had said or what had happened afterwards to her. That she would decide (thanks to her tiredness, dull headache, plus the dripping rain still coming down outside the window, that grey smokey fog down below) to put off saying anything until such time as she felt better and the games and *Sixty Minutes* were through and there was nothing more Mel wanted to watch. That Nancy would call sometime late in the day and they would talk but not about that, not even to Nancy her best friend though she was off in the kitchen where Mel couldn't hear and Marie wasn't back from practice yet. That sure enough, Frank himself would be there at the very next party, the very one she and Nancy would be talking over, planning out on the phone, and the party after that and the party after that, quiet and serious and sometimes laughing through his beard and past his pipe but with never another word about what he had said tonight, until she finally would stop wondering and forget about it too. That the next time it would even cross her mind to ask about Aileen someone would tell her that she had long since moved back east someplace to go into some nursing program, no one knew with her boyfriend or not; and that these pictures of the three of them, this feeling of newness, of swift breeze, of change were like the best part of a story, the peak of excitement just before the ending makes you came back again, and what was really going on as she was lying there was that the whole thing was finally behind her and she was falling back to sleep.

Poker Fugue

Tom Daniels

It was no use, really, trying to get the story across to them, the young men and women back in Cleveland who, like him, wrote company reports and promotional stuff of one stripe or another, who got together with him weekend nights downtown at Leo's Place to talk and drink and listen to the jazz. They would have had to have come from small towns too, which most of them, he imagined, did not. They would have to know what it was like to go back there for days, walled up in your folks' house with grotesque wall-to-wall carpeting and the tv on all the time, in this place you left so far behind, so long ago, the things you recognize about it now, the faces you have to say Hi to seem to come back out of someone else's life.

And the things, the faces you remember, just walking down the street you grew up on, lived your whole life on before college. The little frame houses going down the hill like his parents' but smaller, with no playroom tacked on out back to spoil their lines. All the people living there, the ones you hope never to see again, for you have even less to say to them, with them, than to and with your folks. Old Mrs. Kreps, the piano teacher. The Clarks, the Bronsons, the Mannings, the Fortners, the Danns. Eddy Bronson, wide square sandy-haired kid he could get down on the playground, one of the few, before anybody got to him to wrestle him down into the mud, the snow. Mrs. Kreps, who sometimes after the lesson gave him soup. The creaking, almost regular, of the plant at the bottom of the hill, the squeak of his tread on the snow in dry still air.

He walked past Main Street's Christmas bells blinking red on the road, to the Ideal Bar hard off the west edge of the plant. It was taking a real risk, he knew, but he had to get out of the house. Either that or go back, tell his father to shut up about welfare giveaways and blacks, his mother to stop her endless chattering and deferral to his father, then kick the tv set in.

Inside the Ideal the tv was on, too, over the bar, but of the dozen or so in there, there was nobody he recognized, or who seemed to recognize him. He ordered a brandy and soda, sat at the bar staring up like the others at the set where a black family was camping out, ha ha; then turned his head at the sound of the door and saw Kris Kinney come in.

Kris

Picked up a pitcher and two glasses, went right up and slapped a hand on his back. Well shit, I said, don't say hello or anything Tommy Daniels but how the hell are you? Don't recognize your old friends anymore?

Well, he said, fact of the matter was he didn't know whether *I* recognized him and he didn't want to come up to me and say nothing if I didn't or didn't want to see him. Or some shit like that. Just home for Christmas, he said, had to be getting back soon. Works for some big company in Cleveland. Writes reports for them or some shit. Still single too.

So he asked about me and I told him about the service, Nam and North Dakota and coming back here and getting fixed up with Ann again (which he remembered from high school, which kind of surprised me). And about getting out and coming back here and signing on, five years back now, and the two kids.

Goddamn, he said when I was all through.

So we kept on drinking beer and talking, mostly him asking about this one and that. Bunch of shirttails came in after a while to catch a quick one before the midnight, Georgie Scheer and Billy Carlson and that crowd, about as fucked up stoned as these young guys usually are for work any more, and damn if he didn't recognize them too, though not by name of course, and we played a little team eightball at the quarter table, dollar a game, and that was what got me thinking about poker. How I went up to his place two, three times even, back when he was in college and home on vacation, playing mostly with a bunch of other college guys. They had a real nice table up at his place, and chips, and sometimes his old man, Bob Daniels, he'd play a while too. Funny guy. Usually laughed a lot, didn't know his cards for shit, no more than his boy knew how to shoot stick. Always lost.

So when the shirttails left I asked if he still played, if he was up for a game right now. He said could I get one together at this hour? No problem, I told him, but the truth was it took a while to scare up enough guys off shift tomorrow til the four o'clock anyway who weren't racked out yet. Got Gib out of bed, but that didn't matter to him. Then the only others I could get hold of were just Tanner and goddamn Randy, but there was five anyway. Walked back out front from the phone and he was still there, nursing a cup of Tronetto's coffee. Bought a case of beer from Tronetto, let him pay for it. What the hell, I told him, your game after all. And then we were on our way.

Gib

Gilbert Allen lies there a minute longer, looking up at the ceiling and finishing his cigarette, then eases out slow so as not to wake her up. Takes his clothes off the chair and puts them on out in the hall over his underwear. Goes down into the kitchen, turns the light on. Clock over the sink says Twelvethirty. Jesus. Drag ass tomorrow. In the cupboard he reaches back behind the plates for the house payment envelope. Takes all but twenty, puts it back. Just before he walks out the back door one of the kids in the bedroom off the kitchen says something in her sleep. He stops, waits, listens. Nothing more.

He walks out coatless, trots through the cold to the barn. Two years now, almost, since he cut the midsection of the barn in half by putting up support joints, walling the room with three-quarter-inch plywood. Right now it is cold as hell in there. He turns on the space heater full blast, grabs a beer out of the fridge he got from Nappy on the maintenance crew last summer. Turns on the radio to the Buffalo station, oldies all night. Take it easy, take it easy, don't let the sound of your own wheels drive you crazy. He beats his hands on his jeans. He takes his shaded granny glasses out of the case in his shirt pocket and puts them on, and looks through them at the tits of the lovely stretched out on the beach on the wall across from him. He opens a fresh pack of Marlboros from his other pocket, fishes out his Zippo, looks at it: a hunter shooting at a duck, initials G. A. He lights up. He takes the cards, shuffles them up, deals five off the top. King high. Has to take a whiz. Walks outside.

Looks at his tracks in the snow, across the yard. He remembers Tom Daniels all right. Yeah, shit yes. Few years older than him, big shit in high school. He tries to piss his initials in the snow, G. A.

Tom Daniels

It felt good to be there, in the big gas-eating Ford with its heater blasting, with Kris at the wheel. Stop by home, leave a note for the folks? No, fuck it, he decided. He lolled his head back against the seat and looked over at Kris's rough dark face. "So" he said, smiling, "how you like this car?"

"It's all right. Runs. Gets us where we want to go."

Don't let it drop, he thought: say something else, show you know something he knows. "What kind of mileage you get on it?"

"Shit," Kris said, "I don't know."

It's all right, he thought, it's okay, let it go. He took another slug of beer, looked out at the bright star mounted on the plant 1 smokestack, at the dark hills, at the stars.

"I'll tell you, Tom," Kris said. "What are you now, twenty-nine, same as me, right?"

"Yes," he said, knowing suddenly, with a sickening certainly what was coming, waiting for Kris to start it, reach over and grab him and punch his face in, tell you just what an asshole you truly are and cut this patronizing shit out okay?

"Yeah," Kris said. leaning back from the sheel. "I'll tell you, I had a lot of growing up to do before I could come back here. There was a lot of shit I had to get out of my system. I mean I could have stayed up there in Bismarck watching them missiles and playing cards and made a hell of a lot more than I'll ever get out of this place, you know? But Ann and I, we figure hell, it's our home, you know?"

"So goddammit, Tom," Kris said. looking away from the road, aiming his finger slowly at him: "Don't forget that. You never really leave your goddamn home. You ever think about coming back? You ought to think about coming back."

"I do think about it," he said, surprised at everything, suddenly, drunkenly pleased, keeping his face as grave, as stern as his old friend Kris's was. "Lots of times I think I'd like to come back," he said. "Hell yes."

Kris

Anyway, said he'd think about it. So, time we got out there, I see Tanner's camper in the driveway, Randy's goddamn Firebird about half in the fucking ditch out front, so we just walked back there, set right down and started playing. Came through the door with the case, goddamn Gib don't even look up, just says That all you got? Thought you said you was buying, ain't enough there to get one of us through. Fucking cheap asshole, but I told him just to shut the fuck up, Tommy, he smiled and shook hands all around and we just set right down to play.

Tanner

Tanner frowned a lot, no matter what he was doing. Sometimes he was pretty sure everybody was ready to laugh their ass off at him, or maybe they were even doing it at the time. He couldn't tell, he couldn't figure for sure. Tanner lived with his folks up off the Two Mile. Tanner had his own camper truck with customized shell unit on the back and a mattress inside just in case. In the cab he had his Winchester .30-.30 just in case. Tanner picked his cards up as soon as they came and leaned back in the chair. His back straight, lips puckered, frowning, reading the cards. In the plant sometimes he worked with Gib and Randy and Kris. Loading dock number two. The new guy there beside him, what's his name, smelled like soap. Made him think of pretty women. Look at that one Gib had up on the wall, think about doing it. Tanner reached for the can of beer on the table and picked it up and poured some into his mouth. The first card he got was a three of clubs, next card was a ten of hearts. When he picked it up they told him to leave it back down there, face up. Stud poker this hand was. Five card stud. Tanner nodded when he put the card back down and frowned and didn't say anything and looked around at them in the way he had of doing it so they couldn't tell he was watching them.

Six gets a king. Fours pair. In the bedroom Gib's wife has a dream, of seeing an old friend of hers from high school, Sherrie, who tells her all these kids running in from all sides are yours now and you have to take care of them. The thin bare branches of a chokeberry bush at the edge of the ditch slap against the Firebird's fender, half-buried in snow. King high gets another spade, three showing. The wind rattles the storm windows of the frame house on Ransom Street, where Ann

*and the kids are asleep. In plant 1 Tanner's father works the mid-
night, hot end, blinking at the heat and light as the stuff comes out of
the furnace, wiping his red face on his sleeve. Ten gets an ace. On
Euclid Ave. in downtown Cleveland the all-black cleaning crew is
closing the office back up. Queen gets a deuce, no apparent help. In
Tom Daniels' apartment just off Shaker Square, the digital clock on
the bedside table snaps the minute off.*

Randy

Just throw it out there anyway man, what the fuck's the
difference, Randy throws it out there and then takes another
look at his pitiful motherfucking hand, man, and has to fucking
crack up cause in the first place he is so wasted on that weed and
speed you did on the way out here, man, that the whole thing,
just being here is insane, first of all, but second even he is not so
far fucking gone as not to be able to tell what a miserable mother
fucking hand this is. "Hey wait," he says, giggling, scraping the
whiskers on his chin, jamming the other hand into his jeans, the
wad of bills, "hey fuck it, take it up another dollar," and starts
laughing so hard, so fucked up he damn near falls out of
the chair.

"Well gentlemen, I'm afraid that's a little too rich for my
blood."

Randy stops laughing, the speed energy building, hitting
straight up, sweet rush of the pure fucking fun it would be, is
gonna be to wipe the floor with the fucking asshole who said
that. Yeah. The fucking asshole who sits next to him, what the
fuck's his name, big fucking asshole from out of town, whatever.
"What the fuck you say, asshole?" Randy says smiling, almost
losing it again, waiting for the asshole to say any goddamned
thing at all, make one fucking move and move in and beat the
shit out of him, smash the whole fucking place down, but then
right when he is all set, ready to get it *on*, he sees the way the
poor fucking asshole Tanner is looking at him, that dumb shit,
just *look*ing at him so goddamn stupid he doesn't even know
how fucked up it is, everything that is going on, and that is so
fucking pitiful and you are so wasted, man, that you just fucking
crack up again.

Tom Daniels

At times things felt tense if only because they were playing a dollar and up a card, obviously more than any of them could afford, including him. Then there was this guy Randy, so far gone on something or other, he looked like he could cut your throat if he didn't like the color of your tie. And then Kris too was acting a little strange: somewhere in that first half of the game he beat out Kris's spade flush with a full house, jacks on sixes, and looked up from the money he was stacking and straightening to see Kris's eyes narrowed on him, his cards still in his hand.

"Had you running anyway, huh?" Kris said.

"Sure did," he said, nodding, smiling.

"You pick up the boat on the last card?" Kris said.

"Uh-huh," he said, looking back down at the piles of coin, stack of bills. In fact, he had no idea when the last card had come in, he had already forgotten. "Fool's luck," he said, and self-deprecatingly shrugged.

No one else laughed or spoke. From the corner of his eye he could see Gib Allen's gaze behind the shades flick quickly over him, then move to Kris, then back, as if picking up information on the way. He tried to remember if ever, back in high school, he had ever actually talked or done anything with Gib, or if it was only that sad goat's face he recognized. The Tanner fellow and this crazy Randy he was quite sure he didn't know. Between the space heater and the beer, his whole top half was flushed, while his legs and feet were absolutely numb. He kept his face calm and pleasant and, when he had to look at anyone, for a while smiled off toward Tanner or Gib. He was winning, but not enough to get very far ahead or anything. For the longest time the only sounds came from the radio, the cards and money on the table, the announcements of the final hands, the next games, even crazy Randy had stopped laughing now. Finally, for a while he met every bet no matter how bad his hand was, and no matter how good it was never raised until he was even again or slightly down, at which point he realized that for some time now he had had to take the world's biggest piss.

Stepping outside into the brisk air cleared his head again. He sighed several times, watched the steam float out of his mouth. Suddenly it felt wonderful to be alive; and on the way back in, just outside the door, he had to laugh at the sheer wonderful

craziness of being with these guys back home again, playing all
night for these stakes. Then, through the door, he heard Gib
Allen's dry voice.

"Goddamn," he was saying. "He's having so much fun out
there, he must be playing with it."

When he stepped back inside, smiling tightly, Tanner was still
making a high startled squealing sound, Randy was laughing so
hard tears were breaking down his cheeks, and Kris was shuffling
the deck, smiling back at him.

"Play a little draw," Kris said. "Jacks to open, trips to win.
Change the game a little bit."

Tanner

Tanner turned the cards over he had down on the table. I
have, he said and swallowed. I have three kings and two queens.
Gib said Well you win. Randy said what the fuck was he doing
betting just a dollar on a hand like that. Tanner did not know
what to say. He pulled the money in to him. A second later,
when Randy wasn't looking, Tanner looked at the other guy,
the new one, and frowned and shrugged. The guy gave him a
little smile. The next time starting out Tanner got three red
hearts. When it came around to him Tanner put in the one dol-
lar plus two more. There. But the next one was not another
heart, it was the jack of spades, but that gave him a pair of jacks.
Tanner bet five dollars when it came around to him. It was all he
could do to keep from smiling, inside him it felt like he was run-
ning or laughing or going fast in a car. Tanner reached out and
grabbed another beer and opened her up and looked at all of it
out there on the table and heard the radio, the way the song
went up and up. The next card was a six, a six of diamonds, he
bet five dollars on it, the next card was a four, four of hearts.
Tanner had to reach in his pocket. He bet five dollars, a five dol-
lar bill. This time if he won he would put it in his pocket, that
way he could feel it in there, slap it with his hand , feel its
weight. Maybe buy something with it afterwards. What? Tanner
walking down the street, past stores, with the weight of money,
people looked at Tanner, Tanner did not have to look back.
Next card was a six, another six. Tanner bet five dollars. Every-
body got out but Kris, Kris looked at him and said Okay what
you got. I got a pair of jacks and a pair of sixes, Tanner said. Kris
threw his cards down on the table over the money and said Shit.

Tanner's knees were jiggling up and down, fast. Kris said Well you got it then. Tanner picked up all his cards and smacked them down and jumped up to push the money over, all the stuff inside coming up in this throat and mouth, coming out, Eat *that* motherfuckers, Tanner said, grinning, shouting his stretched mouth, not seeing them at all.

Kris

That's just exactly why I never played much over in Nam, dumb shits like that, right there. Get in a game with some dumb fuck doesn't know dick shit what he's doing, you can't play cards, can't bluff worth a goddamn, no matter what they'll stay. Then ones like Randy, crazy bastards high as kites, go out on patrol they're just as likely to blow you away as Charlie, half the time he's so fucked up it's a wonder he doesn't run somebody over with the goddamn forklift down there the way he wheels that thing around, laughing, it's a wonder anything gets done down there. They ought to can their asses, all them dopers like that. I mean, I got no time for them at all.

No, the person I felt sorry for there after a while was Tommy, the way that poor sonofabitch kept going up against him. Goddamn Randy was too, of course, going up against Tanner, but that's his business what he does. Thing is, you can't go against streaking dumb luck like that. You got to just stay back, wait for it to piss away, have a beer and bide your time. But old Tommy, though, he damn near lost everything there about three, three-thirty, four. One time right after he'd got blown away again, I was watching him, he pulled everything he had left out of his wallet, there was just about ten dollars was all. And I looked over at him and said, you know, How's it going? This what you wanted, you doing all right? Damn poor card player, you know, but you got to hand it to him, he was a real good loser, acted real good about the whole thing, never said a damn word the whole time.

Randy

Rubs a cold shaking had over his forehead, old greasy speedsweat there. Maybe a joint to smooth things out. Fumbling in his coat. Someone saying his name. "Huh?" "What do you have?" He looks, remembers, shit. "Two pair, kings and tens." "I got a flush, queen high." Closes his eyes, his dry

mouth, yawns. One hand still searches in his pocket, comes out
with a joint. Reaches for Gib's lighter, lights up. His eyes meet
Kris's. He takes a long toke, down deep, opens his eyes. God-
damn, how much money you dropped? "Anybody for a hit?" he
says, holding it up. "Get that shit out of here," Kris says. He
holds it out to Tanner, smiling. "Want a hit, Steve?" Tanner gig-
gles like a girl. Little rushes lick at Randy's insides, his vision
blurs as he holds out the joint Kris takes out of his hand and,
standing, going to the door, throws out. The cold air comes
across the room, hits him all over, like his whole body hurts. "I
told you I don't want that shit around me," Kris says, sitting
down.

Randy is still standing, closing his eyes. Ought to break the
pusgut motherfucker's ass. Turn the table over and follow it, cut
the motherfucker a new asshole. But shit man. He is so wasted,
so far gone. And working the four o'clock yet today, no shit man
you're gonna need that goddamn money now, gotta show for it
now for sure. Trailer rent, fucking car payment, goddamn den-
tist, stereo, cb . . .

Randy reaches behind him for his coat. "Shit," he says. "Piss
on you. All you fuckers. Fuck it man." Slides what's left off the
table, puts it back in his jeans, fishes out another j and, quick,
grabs Gib's lighter, lights up again. Deep toke. "Check you later,
assholes."

Little light there is already coming over the hills hurts the hell
out of his eyes, but the cold air smooths the high. On the way to
the car he shivers like a bastard. Better get your ass to bed, man,
catch some sleep before the fucking four o'clock. So the guy's an
asshole, so what. They're all assholes, what the fuck.

*Five card stud, seven stud. WKBW, bringing you the hits of yes-
terday and yesteryear for all you nightowls out there.*

*Say, listen, hey we don't have far to go, huh? Just a few more hours
and that old man sun gonna be hauling his head up for the rosy down,
pretty poetic huh? So just to get us to it on this cold cold Thursday
morning in the dark we're gonna take some heat from all the way
back in 1972, the great Rod Stewart, remember Maggie Mae, from
KB, taking you back for the best . . .*

*Draw, jacks to open, trips to win. All I need, is the air, that I
breathe, and to love you. Can't have you, I don't want nobody baby.
Clear and cold, with thirty percent chance of some precipitation later*

in the day, and a warming trend moving down. Tanner is moved to plant 1, foreman, his father dies, Kris gets a divorce and moves up to foreman, loading dock, Daniels becomes promotional head for the northeast region, Randy is fired, goes through bankruptcy, works at the Esso station, disappears, Gib stays the same. Cincinnatti, three in your hand, five on the table, bets on each one.

Tom Daniels

Finally, once Randy the bad-ass was gone, everything was okay. He had something of a headache, and the radio's idiot shit got on his nerves sometimes, and at least a part of him wished that Randy had started something before leaving so that he could have watched Kris push his face in. But at least the guy was gone, and the rest of them were together the way you can only be together after you've been playing cards a long, long time.

He and Gib were coming up slow, and Kris was winning again. "Guess that evens us up, huh?" Kris said at one point, when he beat out his trip jacks with a flush; and it took a long moment for him to remember that full boat that beat Kris's other flush, it already seemed so long ago, so far in the past.

"Yeah, sure," he said, genuinely smiling and chuckling. "Even steven, Kris."

Gib

Close to even, very close. "Seven stud," he says. "And let's make it the last round."

Tanner says nothing, he is slumped back half asleep. The Daniels guy nods, Kris says "Yeah sure." "Say Gib," says Daniels. "Would you mind if I stole one of your cigarettes?"

He snaps the pack with his index finger so it shoots across the table to him, and deals.

After him Tanner deals seven stud again, the Daniels guy deals Cincinnatti, Kris deals jacks to open, trips to win and bets the pot way up. They go five hands and on the sixth Gib pulls three eights on the draw and hauls it in, the whole house payment, maybe more. Inside, he feels the tightness letting go, like a long cold drink going down. But he keeps his face the same.

After the last hand Kris has him co-sign a marker on what Tanner owes him, $275 plus interest, 10% a month. Tanner takes off. The Daniels guy says he is only down about thirty, so it was just Randy and Tanner who got blown away. Kris is feeling like King Shit, says Why don't we all go down to the bakery, catch some breakfast there?

When he stands the ache in his ass comes alive, moves down his legs. Outside, by the car, he looks over at the house. One time when he was a kid, the old man didn't come home from the plant this one night when he was supposed to, and he figured it out from something his old lady said and that night he kept on waking up and thinking about it. After a while he snuck out of bed and went over and started looking out the window at the streetlight, waiting for his old man to show up in it. Which would never have happened anyway unless he happened to be walking for some reason, because he'd smashed the car up or something. But this one time he still sat there a good while, thinking the old man'd show up out there in that light.

In his house now all the windows are dark. In the car he passes two smokes to them, lights the last for himself and leans back, smoking up at the roof. Course she won't be any too happy when she does get up and finds him still out, out all night. Too late to worry about it now though, is the way he figures it. Too late to worry about it now.

Kris

So I told him straight out, I said you think I was hard on that cocksucker, I'll tell you. I'd never see it if I didn't charge interest on the sonofabitch, and Gib here'll back me up on that.

Then I asked him if that wasn't just about the best goddamn sausage he ever had. He said he had to agree with me about that. We had eggs and sausage and coffee and the whole thing, you know. Being big winner and all, I sprung. Then, anyway, about the time we get up to leave, old Borowski and Miller drag in off the midnight, ask us what the hell we're doing down there. And Gib he just looks the way he does, not cracking a smile, and says Oh we get up nice and early today. We want to go down, pick out our goddamn free Christmas turkey. And of course we all get a good laugh out of that.

So then I wheeled old Tommy over to his place. And I told him one more time, I said Listen, why the hell you want to live out in Cleveland anyway?

Sure, old Gib says, when you could work with us down at the plant.

We all had to laugh at that too, of course, but I told him too,

I said you remember what we were talking about. I want to see
you here goddammit, okay?

He said he'd remember. He wouldn't forget.

And the next time you get back here, I told him, you call me
up, I'll fix you up with the best goddamn fucking poker game
you ever played, okay?

And he said you fucking A.

And so we let him off, Then we did end up going down to the
plant after all. See, all this time I'd been thinking how it
wouldn't be a bad idea if I did go down, pick up my goddamn
turkey after all. How I'd look showing up bright and early with
the money in my goddamn pocket and the turkey in my hand.
Old Gib, course he said fuck it, he wasn't gonna stand in line up
at the from office, suck anybody's ass. He just sat out there in
the car, wouldn't even come in while I went up where Mr. Wal-
lin was handing them out and got mine. Course, sooner or later
he'll come get his too, he'll come sucking around. And I was
right too, it did just tickle the shit out of old Ann.

Tanner

Tanner's father was in the kitchen. Where you been? Playing
cards, Tanner said. I was out playing cards with some guys. Tan-
ner's father kept on eating. Fried potatoes, ketchup. How'd you
do, he said. Tanner said All right. Tanner's father finished and
went out. Tanner sat down in the same chair for a while. Tan-
ner's father came back in with his shirt off and asked him when
he worked next. Tanner said four o'clock today. Tanner's father
went back out. Tanner sat there a while longer, then got up and
took the plate to the sink and started to run some water over it
but stopped. The thought of eating made him sick. He walked
into the front room. Tanner's mother was on the couch putting
on her shoes. The tv was on, a game show where people win
money. Tanner went into the bedroom. Bruce and Joe were still
asleep but Shirley was awake. She sat on the bed and looked at
him. Tanner did not look at her back. He thought of saying
when you damn kids going back to school, but didn't. Tanner's
mother called her in a minute to go feed the chickens anyway.
Tanner dropped back and laid himself out on the bed and slept a
while. When he woke up he took his boots off. Bruce and Joe
were gone. Ten per cent, Tanner whispered. He started taking
his shirt off but then instead got into bed with all his clothes still

on and was asleep again.

Tom Daniels

"A card game." Speaking softly, moving down the hall towards his room.

Sound of water running, then his father's voice again: "Who with?"

"You remember Kris Kinney?" he said, his fingers numbly working at the buttons of his shirt. "Came up a few times when we used to play here?"

"Oh yeah," his father said after a second. "Sure. Art Kinney's boy."

"Yeah. He's married to Ann Dunn now, has a couple kids." He picked up his clothes and walked down the hall to the bathroom. His father, too, was in his underwear, lathering his face at the sink, but moved aside ot let him by to the laundry basket, then to stand beside him to brush his teeth. "Him and a couple of other guys."

"Jesus," his father said. "You smell like a brewery."

He laughed. "Feel like one too."

"So how'd you do?" his father said.

He bent to spit before answering and suddenly felt his stomach rolling over, all the beer, cigarettes, eggs and that greasy hot sausage and the sicky-sweet bakery smells gushing up hot in his throat. Jesus, right in front of Dad. He stood up, swallowed it back.

"Pretty well, I think, considering. I lost about thirty. But jesus, they were playing like five bucks a card."

His father leaned closer to the mirror, stroking the razor along his throat. "*You're* not making enough to be playing at those stakes."

"I know it," he said. "I was scared to death the whole time."

"And you wonder why they can't pay their bills at the end of the month," his father said, sighing.

"You'd better get yourself to bed," called his mother drowsily from his parents' bedroom. "You'd better get some sleep."

"Yeah." Then again, just as swiftly, the impulse to gag; so hard this time he rocked backwards with it, forcing it down. When his eyes opened again his father was smiling at him in the mirror.

"Well," his father said, "I guess you're probably just about as piss-poor a poker player as your old man."

"Yeah," he said, smiling back. "Probably am."

His father finished shaving, rinsing the sink out, carefully combed his thin hair. "You're waiting to use the shower or something, go ahead," he said. "I'll be out of here in a minute, I've got to get down to the store."

"Fine. Thanks." But already he had decided to skip the shower now, get one later when he woke up. Take the sheets and throw them in the laundry then too. So in another minute he was in his bedroom again, standing chilled and naked on the hardwood floor, looking out the window, down at the part of town it showed, the plumes rising from the chimney, from his father's car pulling out of the driveway, down the road, and from the smokestack of the plant with its red Christmas star against the hills. And he felt fine about being home, back with his parents in the town he'd grown up in. Even then he knew, though, it was no use telling the story to the others, his buddies down at Leo's back in Cleveland. They would never understand the full significance of it, what it all really meant to him.

The Fame of Price

The Chamber of Commerce man who interviews him for the job has a round, grim face on a half-bald head with sparse black hairs combed straight back. When Price enters the small office he is slumped back frowning in his fake leather chair, looking almost as tired and luckless as the other, younger men Price has just left thumbing through back issues of *The American Legion* in the reception room out front. Price does his number dutifully, extending his hand and bright clean smile along with his bland name, and the man's head snaps up with narrowed eyes as he grapples Price's hot, sweaty hand across the desktop, muttering "Ed Granelli" as they shake.

Granelli, Granelli, wonders Price as he sits: now what kind of store would he have? Men's Clothes he'd say if he had to take a guess. Meanwhile Ed Granelli dourly runs his eyes over the application as though it were the menu in the restaurant where he ate lunch everyday. This is always the moment Price worries most about, for fear they'll ask him what he's doing here, a college graduate and all that. But Granelli's question is a standard opener he could have picked up in a noontime Rotary talk designed to make him hip: "So tell me, John. What makes you want to be a temporary Santa in our little town?"

I need the money. And don't call me John. But of course Price keeps his smile on and hitches himself forward, kicking into gear. "Well sir" – a calculated gesture in itself – "I like people; and I especially enjoy working with children – "

He lets it run, lets the bilge flow out, and two minutes later Granelli is nodding in agreement, though the sour frown stays on. When Price stands up to go, he stands up too, offering his hand first for the final shake; then, at the instant of triumph, the round face crumples into a grimace at Price's frame. "You sure you gonna be able to look fat enough?" Granelli says.

"No problem," beams Price. "I pad real well."

He almost always does get the job in cases·like this, when you just come in off the street, fill something out, and walk into the next room. Once, back in the California days, just out of school with his brand-new, useless Liberal Arts degree, he scored his best, longest-lasting, highest-paying one this way, a stint as a sort of editorial assistant in an outpost of a seedy educational publishing firm. For almost two years before the recession bit in, he fractured long sentences and substituted small words for large, rendering dull prose into garble at the right readability level for deprived adolescents until he could and sometimes did perform these mangling in his sleep – and all because one sunny spring afternoon he had felt suddenly nervy, walked unheralded into the first office he saw, and asked with the right sort of intelligent good cheer for an application and a job. And now for nigh on to three years, ever since leaving California to pursue a plump vegetarian fiddler named Sylvia up here to Corvallis, Oregon, where his degree is even more of a joke, his life has been a series of temporary assignments. So far, the same pleasantness that allows him to form new relationships with women has also been able to get him new short-term jobs as shoe salesman, motel desk clerk, etc.: until finally Price has come to think of practically everything, even Sylvia herself (who, along with her commune, spurned him long ago as a hopeless carnivore) as no more than a trick of that same fate which has just led him through this newest door to the next job, out of his quite palpable fear of being enslaved in a plant or jobless, and unloved.

PRICE TO PORTRAY SANTA CLAUS IN XMAS MARKETPLACE

Halfway home, when the headline flashes through his mind, he laughs out loud in the Oregon drizzle, feeling the tension give way. Two months since he has kicked in any money for the food or rent to Susan; six months since the last job. That alone is enough to explain the strain between them lately: less lovemaking less good, less talking, short quarrels over nothing at all. It will be good, be fun to tell her about both the headline and the job.

PRICE AND SUSAN SALVAGED BY SANTA GIG

"Oh really?" says Susan, peering up over her reading glasses at him. "And just how long have you been seeing these headlines,

Mr. Price?"

Price laughs easily and steps over the lesson plans strewn around the side of the floor mattress doubling as couch and bed. He bends to kiss her smooth cool forehead, kneels and reaches under her flannel shirt to smooth his hand across her long bare back; he kisses her shoulder, then buries his head in the dark, fragrant space of neck, shoulder and hair. Susan does not react. "Since the day we vurst met I haff always known I vas destined vor greatness vith you by my side," he says, straight off the top of his head.

Susan sits up and turns, searching through the papers for her shoes: mouth set, mirth gone. When she bends over, a sweep of long brown hair falls and obscures her face from him. "I'm going to work a while at the kitchen table, I've got to get these lesson plans done now," she says, and waves one hand towards the red and white costume piled on the chair: "You're going to need some help getting that on tomorrow, aren't you?"

She is twenty-two, younger than him by six years. But when she talks at him like this it is as though she were the caretaker, the older, authoritative one; and she has been putting that tone on more and more these days, with their relationship still not quite one year old. She stands now, with the papers firmly nestled in her arms, the room so dim in late afternoon that he can barely make out the contours of the pretty, frowning face he smiles at. "Yes thanks," Price says simply, quietly. "I guess I am."

A brief pause follows. Could she be thinking the same things he is? Price wonders, staring at what he can still see of her. How dumb the job really is, how stupid he is really going to feel?

"Sweetheart," says Susan softly, "I'm glad you got the job."

"So am I," says Price and stands to hold her as another headline forms and flashes forth to his surprise.

PRICE AS SANTA SMASH HIT

He is less sanguine at ten of eight the next morning, of course, standing on the sidewalk outside the little trailer downtown, waiting for Granelli to come by and open up. Through the display windows of the nearest store, The Clothes Tree, Price can see the skeptical and worse amusement of the saleswomen in their classy outfits, hanging up new blouses on the racks, while from city hall a few blocks away floats the dismal, distorted strain of "O Come All Ye Faithful" played over bad speakers too loud. The steady mist drifting down from flat grey sky has dampened his white plastic hair and beard into clammy, bunched filaments, his head feels stuffed with the same cotton batting he has, with Susan's help, layered over his skinny trunk, and what he sees when he tucks his head and peers down at himself looks like a vision of red foothills, a bad acid flash.

PRICE AS SANTA BUTT OF UNIVERSE

Granelli pulls up at a few minutes of eight, jumps out of his Mercury Montego breathing hard, as if fresh from exercise or a fight with the wife and kids, and gives Price his final instructions fast, apparently without noticing how ridiculous he looks. "Here's the key, don't lose it cause there's no spare, and no dicking around here off hours and at night. Inside is the poster with the cards you hang out over the door, and don't forget to change the days. And don't use the space heater in there too much, o-kay? This thing is already costing us an arm and a leg – "

SANTA'S HQ! the sign proclaims in magic marker capitals, alternating red and green; then, in smaller letters, Come and Tell Santa What you Want! Only ＿＿ more Shopping Days til Christmas! with the number, from 15 to 1, to be taped on each day. The trailer inside is as cool and damp as a stone cellar. Price hangs the poster on its hook along the outside front, jacks the box-sized heater all the way up, settles his foreign bedraggled self down in the captain's chair where passersby will be able to see in, and waits. Soon it is clear that he will have to decide whether to look back or not at the men and women going past outside to shop or work, who regard him more or less uniformly with the opaque gazes of people on a fast trip through a zoo. Directing his pleasant smile back at them, which he does for a while, has no effect on their blank stares; staring straight ahead himself through the trailer's tiny, murky front window at the sporadic oncoming traffic, yet still feeling those looks, is in some ways even worse. Price opts for the latter course, though, finally, and devotes himself to the wavering car-shapes and to completely, utterly, emptying out his mind. Only fifteen shopping days. Then you can do something else.

PRICE'S ABSURDITY DEEPENS
LOWEST LIFE FORM CURRENTLY ON DISPLAY·

"Go on," a woman is saying. "I'll wait out here."

And Price emerges from his cloud of unknowing to the sight of a young housewife standing outside looking pointedly down the street and away, while a ruddy little boy, his brown eyes glazed with avarice and fear, peers through the door. "Santa?" says the little boy in a tense whisper. "Is that really you?"

"Uh-huh," Price says, nodding slowly. "It's really me all right. You want to come over here and climb up on my lap?" And, as the boy steps in and walks towards him solemnly, perhaps even with a touch of awe, Price feels his heart shuddering with such pain and joy, it is all he can do to keep himself from snatching up the boy in his arms and covering his face with kisses, it takes all that he has to not cry.

PRICE BRINGS HOLIDAY CHEER, HOPE, TO DOZENS

"Jesus," Susan says down the hallway in the kitchen, lifting her wry, beautiful face from her work. "It's Santa Claus, dragged in by the cat."

And the opening lines of his stories stick in his throat, along with his low-key glee; Price pulls off the dripping beard and wig and tosses them at the radiator across the front room, strips off the rest of the costume and leaves it right there in a heap.

"Smells like you made dinner," he says.

She pushes the papers away and stands as he walks through the front room to the kitchen; and they kiss and hug. "The cabbage and sour cream thing?" he says; and feels her head nod against his.

They eat the soup casserole out of bowls: it is good and tasty and nourishing and, as usual, Price wishes they had enough money to eat meat, even hamburger, every night instead. Susan seems to go at hers with a more sincere, wholehearted appetite; she smells her bowl and leans back moaning before diving in. At times Price suspects that her relish for such fare is mainly a function of an unconscious assumption that they — or at least she — will not be eating it forever. And if, as they eat and the clock-radio's bad news floats out around them, Price feels impelled to watch her eager gestures, even to reach over to touch the soft down of her arm, smooth curve of her cheek, it is at least partly because he too figures she will not.

For now, though, he is telling her about what happened today, what it was like, and she is telling him on the basis of her student teaching Yes she knows all about the computerized games and toys, it's all her second graders at the Ed School talk about too, and they trade a few funny lines delivered by the kids in their respective worlds and laugh; and Price slides easily into the moment, happy together with her, putting their dishes to soak while she finishes some course plans, then rolls and lights a joint. Then they are in the bedroom, giggling in ludicrous excitement as they strip.

PRICE AND SUSAN COUPLE

But something is bothering him, after all; for here is Susan smoothly under, over, all around him, his own body straining to touch back, and yet behind everything, even the nice dinner and the day on the new job, lies this stupid head game he has to stop playing

PRICE AND SUSAN COUPLE AS THOUSANDS WATCH

for already it has begun to fill him with the same fascinated, self-loathing boredom he used to feel back in high school when, having learned the keyboard, he could not keep the imaginary fingers in his head from typing out every word he thought or saw. God, when was the last time you thought of that?

PRICE CLAIMS MEMORY RETURN THROUGH DRUGS

Stop that! He is looking straight into Susan's beautiful fierce green eyes, in the middle of their lovemaking, listening to her pleasure sounds and making a few of his own; and at the same time wondering what will happen next, thinking how he has no idea how this will all come out. Thirty years from now will he be lying on his back in some crawling flophouse bed inhaling unfiltered cigarettes that make you erupt in coughing fits of liquid sounds, chunks of lung hacked up into the stale dirty air while you lie there waiting only for the next welfare check to arrive?

PRICE DEAD IN TOTAL OBSCURITY

But Price realizes this picture is only taken from some film, for he hates cigarettes and there is no image for the kind of decline and disintegration, the solitude, indignity and death you will have to undergo. Besides, here in the present, events are taking shape that do lead to a predetermined end. "Oh love," he says to Susan, holding her face in his hands; and then, even after they have rolled apart and away, arms touching only along their sides, for a while he is no longer in the headlines.

"Price?" Susan says langorously, just above a whisper. "Back when you were going to school, what did you think you'd do when you got out?"

Price puts his arms behind his head, and looks up at the ceiling, pondering his reply. "It was different then," he says, staring into the dark. "The late sixties, early seventies. It didn't seem like you had to think about it that much."

"But you must have had some idea," Susan says.

"No," he says, "really I didn't."

And suddenly, back in the world, he has something to get across to her. "It wasn't like now," he says, propping himself up on an elbow. "You didn't need a goddamn strategy for your whole life. If you went to college and you stayed out of the draft and Viet Nam, it was just like twenty-four hour gas stations on the freeways or something, you know? You were probably going to get some kind of decent job eventually. Things were going to be all right for you."

Susan tips her head back on the pillow and exhales a sigh. For a silent moment her face floats, pale and opaque, before his eyes; and there is no way he can tell what that sigh and her signless expression mean, what she is thinking of herself or him.

PRICE'S FUTURE UNCERTAIN

"Know what?" she says finally. "I'd like to take a walk. You want to go for a walk with me?"

It is an old habit, almost a tradition with them, since that first night together when they rose in love and laughing from the bed and walked the sun up the length of the town. Since that time last January their walks have grown shorter, of course, more frequent and not necessarily tied to lovemaking before or after; but the action of walking down glimmering wet sidewalks, not talking, alone in the night, has a power still to put them back together. Or at least Price hopes it does, and imagines from the tone of her voice that she does too. So by way of answering, he is up from the mattress gathering their clothes, holding hers out to her.

Outside, for the moment, the rain has stopped. They walk north, between downtown and the university where she goes to school and student-teaches, through a mixture of student housing and private homes, over slick and sopping yellow walnut leaves. The dope is wearing off now, shading into fatigue, but Price still feels the tension too, walking beside her, waiting for the two of them to feel together, be together again, so quiet that between footfalls he is almost certain he can hear her breathe. And is she, is Susan waiting for the same thing?

"Look," she whispers, stopping still.

Price follows her gaze to a bungalow's front window with two people, a couple inside, bathed in the ghostly silver of the tv. The woman, sitting in the armchair almost directly facing them, wears a bathrobe big enough to be the man's, and brushes her wet curly hair. The square-headed man on the couch turns his head from the tv, removes his cigarette, smiles and speaks to her, and she smiles back. Their faces flicker as the shot changes on the tv so that they seem to be inside some early, soundless, primal movie. When the woman faces forward, out towards them, Price turns back to Susan, whose eyes are still fixed on the scene, whose long straight hair tosses in the light breeze, making shadows move across her face. He puts his arm around her, feeling a sudden, exhausted despair.

"Let's go home," he says, as lightly as possible; and, in another second, she nods and turns back with him.

PRICE'S FUTURE "UNCERTAIN AT BEST"

In the days that follow, the headlines abate somewhat, perhaps because he is so busy. The women and kids start forming lines in the rain outside the trailer, leaving him by six o'clock haunted, delighted, drained by the amount of raw desire that has passed through him. One girl at least six years old wants a Barbie doll so badly that her excitement wets her pants and his. A set of towheaded twins come in and run around the trailer, screaming with their arms out at their sides by way of demonstrating the wonder of the computerized fighter jets they crave, while another little boy, aged four or five, in a faded flannel shirt, patched jeans, torn sneakers, mumbles to Santa only that he wants some oranges and a toy gun, and slides away.

"You know what's funny to me?" he says to Susan one noontime when she has joined him for lunch. "These kids are pretty realistic. They don't ask for all that much more than what their families can give them. It's weird, the way they just seem to know."

Susan looks over at him from Santa's chair, which she now occupies, still chewing her tomato and cheese sandwich. "That's a pretty big generalization," she says. "You're not going out there and asking those people how much money they make, are you?"

"No," says Price, "but you can tell. One kid's in clean pressed clothes and his mother's waiting outside in a little blazer and some pumps with an umbrella over her head. Another kid comes in with holes in his knees and pants too big for him, and his mother's out there in an old army coat. And the first kid wants a lot, and the second one doesn't. That's all I'm saying."

"There are a lot of pretty well-off people who don't like to get dressed up," Susan says. "You can't go by that."

"Maybe not," says Price. "But it seems to work out, so I do."

He smiles, thinly. Her mouth grimaces, twisting to the side. But then they both look back down at their sandwiches again.

PRICE AND SUSAN ON THE ROCKS

It is the first time he has flashed a headline in days, almost a week; yet the night after, it happens again, and worse. Maggie, an old roommate of Susan's, and her husband Rob have asked them over for dinner with another couple, a stocky sharp-eyed woman Maggie works with at the phone company and her husband, a draftsman named Earl. The mood in the house is festive, the main course is sweet-and-sour chicken, and so Price finds himself talking perhaps more than he should, telling them how interesting kids are, the way they can place their wishes in the right price range, tag them to the proper brand names, Tonka trucks, Mattel everything, Star Wars, Farrah Fawcett-Majors, Six Million Dollar Man, and what a trip it all is while the rest of them, Maggie and Karen and Rob and Earl smile and laugh, until Susan's voice, pitched high in impatience, comes through.

"I can't *believe* you, Price," she says; and turns smoldering eyes to the rest of them, trying to smile. "I come down to eat lunch with this guy and he's sitting there jiggling these kids in his lap, having the time of his life. Now all he can tell you is what's wrong with them."

"I didn't say anything was wrong with them," says Price, keeping his own smile on despite the heat creeping into his face.

PRICE AND SUSAN SPLIT GROWS

"You're saying they're controlled, manipulated zombies," Susan says. "You have all this fun with them and then turn around and laugh at them behind their backs, and I think it's just plain cynical."

Instead of answering, Price picks up his tumbler of white wine and takes a drink. Then, next to him, Karen leans forward, rolling her eyes. "You want to get cynical," she says brightly, "you ought to go to work for Pacific Bell. That'll do it in no time."

"Amen," says Maggie over the fresh cigarette she is striking up. "Listen, anybody want more chicken? There's plenty more."

"You really do like the kids though, don't you?" says Karen, turning to him with a coaxing, happy voice. "Did you ever think of being a teacher too, like Susan? I mean, then you two could go to work together and everything."

"Nope," Price says, suppressing the thought of those green, yellow walls, scrape of chalk, coats and ties, recess monitoring, more people passing through his ineffectual life. "Never have," he says, grinning amiably back. "Maybe I should, though.'

FAME OF PRICE TUMBLES IN SLOW TRADING
PRICE ON ROCKS

Rob puts his beer down, snorting. "What do you think, Earl? Can you see this guy as a teacher? Mr. Price of the third grade?"

"Don't know," Earl says between steady forkfuls, pokerfaced. "Couldn't say. Maybe so, maybe not."

In the pause that follows he does not dare to look again at Susan. Finally, at the head of the table their hostess jabs her cigarette in her plate, flutters a hand back through her hair. "Well," Maggie says. "Anybody besides me want to smoke a little dope?"

"Sure," says Price. "Everybody must get stoned," while thinking I am not cynical, I am not cynical, please don't go.

PRICE PLEADS INNOCENT TO CYNICISM CHARGE

"All right," says Susan later, back at the apartment, breaking the silence as if in response to something someone has just said. "All right, I'm sorry. You're not cynical. There's nothing cynical about you at all."

Across the room, stretched out on the mattress, Price briefly looks up from the orange he is concentrating on peeling. "Thank you," he says as he pulls the first segments apart, thus creating an amazingly large, ugly, ripping sound.

"You're a very caring person," Susan says from over in her brown armchair. "A very nice guy. It's the first thing anybody picks up on with you, how nice you are."

He turns his head, and can see through the venetian blinds a few feet off the vague, divided reflection of his face, looking stupid and old as a monkey's, sucking and chewing its section of orange against the dark. "Thank you," he says again.

"God damn you," says Susan as she stands, crosses the room, and slaps his shoulder. "What are you *doing,* god damn it? What is the *matter* with you?"

Price drops the orange as he rises, and takes her in his arms as she begins to cry. "I don't know what's wrong with you, John," she says in weary wails between her sobs. "I don't know what you are."

Softly Price kisses her hair. "Maybe that's the problem," he suggests.

And feels her pushing hard, tearing away. "How the hell," she says, red-faced, almost shouting, "how can you just stand there and *say* things like that all the time?"

Practice, thinks Price; then wishes he could cut his mind out of his head.

"My parents," Susan is saying, still breathlessly, "my parents were right. I hate to say it but they are."

PARENTS' SUSPICIONS OF PRICE CONFIRMED

"You're not really a bum," she says. "But you do live here in my apartment and you don't do anything and there's nothing you want to do and you're just so negative all the time and I'm really sorry, Price, but sometimes I can't stand it, I really can't."

He takes a step toward her. She waves him away, sobbing again. He bends down for the orange on the mattress instead. He makes his fingers pull of another section and put it in his mouth, where he swallows it virtually whole. What is this about her parents, what have they been telling her and how? By letters read in secret, phone calls when he is not around?

PARENTS NIX PRICE FOR SUSAN

SUSAN NIXES PRICE

PRICE NIXED

Susan blows her nose fiercely, green eyes glaring straight at him. Price puts yet another segment in, though chewing it feels very awkward, time-consuming and unnatural with her looking at him like that.

"In another month," she says, "I'm done with student teaching. Then I'm going to get a real job."

He swallows with some difficulty. It is clear what he is now supposed to say. "So," he says, "you want me to move out?"

PRICE CUTS THROAT AS THOUSANDS CHEER

For a long instant they are looking at each other: simply seeing, nothing more. Then her face takes on a definite expression, soft and relaxed. She steps over, slips her arms around his waist and gives him a full, firm kiss, tongue and all. "We can still see each other, can't we?" she says. "You've got enough money to find yourself a place, don't you? Why don't we stay together through Christmas anyway?"

"Sure," says Price to whichever question it is, and holds her close to him. Closer. Tighten up. He turns and looks for their reflection in the window, but cannot find it. More or less simultaneously he wonders whether he has really ever had a real feeling in the last five years or so, and how much, how long this one is going to hurt.

"Come on," Susan whispers, breaking with him again, taking his hand and leading him over to the mattress. "Whatever you want, Love," says Price.

PRICE GOES ON

December 23rd (Only 2 more Shopping Days til Christmas!), in the middle of what even more pointedly now promises to be his last week with Susan: all talking over but the most functional, tiptoeing through the evenings as if someone next door were dying, curled up back to back like bookends on the mattress, careful not to touch at any moment of their last fitful faintly-shared sleeps. Already this morning, this day promises to be the worst so far: his sick sadness constantly here like a rising choking pool in his chest. "And I want a *real* bike, a ten-speed," says the blond snub-nosed boy, much too big and old for Price's lap. "And a pro football pong game. Really any kind of game's okay, as long as it's computerized."

"Okay," says Price. "That's fine, Jimmy. Is that everything now?"

"You got tears in your eyes," says the boy, sliding down. "There isn't any Santa Claus, is there?"

"Merry Christmas to you now," says Price, smiling, standing, opening the trailer to the drizzle outside. "May I have your attention please?" he calls out to the line of kids and mothers trailing down the block. "We're going to have to close down here for a very short time, but Santa will be right back."

A few minutes later, over on Second Street, he is inside the Peacock Bar. The beard and wig are both off, sitting on the bartop, and although the three older men he shares the bar with have a hard time not smirking, nobody is saying a word about the red padded suit, not even the barkeep. On the first whiskey his empty stomach almost goes up to his mouth, but the second and third warm and light him better than he has felt for days. Soon, from the great pocket of clarity which has opened in his skull, that comfortable warm darkness, he can hear his own voice talking over the c-w on the jukebox and the knock of billiard balls, speaking now, it would seem, to the man down the bar to his right.

bar to his right.

"Plenty others," says the man when he pauses for breath. "Wouldn't kill myself if I was you."

The man is right, of course, but the words are coming out now and Price cannot stop. He is telling the guy about one of those others, this woman Carol, real nice person he went with once, even nicer than Susan maybe, how he saw her in line a couple days ago and here she's married some guy works at the chemical plant, got a kid and everything, little girl three years old, crawled right up on his lap, told him everything she wanted just like all the rest of them, now how about that?

"That's something all right," says the man down the bar to his right.

"You think that's something?" Price says grinning, with the stinging in his eyes again. "How bout this? How about these stupid headlines I been seeing right up to last week when things fell apart and they stopped, how bout that?" he says, laughing again, shoulders heaving with it.

The man down the bar looks around as if embarrassed; then back over at Price's head lowered against the bar. "Hey buddy," he says. "Hey son, buck up." Then, louder: "Can we have another double shot here, please?"

"No no," says Price, sliding his hand down his face, easing his body off the stool. "Better be getting back."

And the funny thing is, he does feel better or at least less bad, moving back through the crowd on the sidewalks outside. Only the light seems at all troublesome in its intensity now, a dazzling overcast whiteness evenly dispersed across the sky and through the air, an almost painful radiance sharpening all it falls on, even Granelli whose tight red face he sees as soon as he rounds the corner on Madison, Granelli on the trailer steps, up at the head of the line, Granelli's mouth opening and closing, talking to the kids and mothers, trying to form something like a smile.

Then Granelli has caught sight of him, and is walking over fast. They will meet near the end of the trailer, Price figures; and is cheered to find that though his heart is pounding, his sense of distance is intact. Then Granelli's fiery face is next to his.

"What is the meaning of this?" Granelli is saying. "I come down here to give you your check, find the place locked up and you off boozing it up. We don't have to stand for this, I'll tell you, I don't care how close to Christmas – "

And yet beyond the sound of that voice is still the brightness, the clarity, the distance: already one of Price's hands is pulling on the plastic beard and wig, while the other brushes Granelli's chest, waving him out of the way. "Mr. Granelli," Price is saying, "you are a complete asshole," as he moves steadily, steadily beyond Granelli and through the crowd and up the trailer steps.

The light still hurts his eyes, the blood aches in his brain; and both sensations are welcome, nonetheless. There will be more jobs after this one, other loves besides Susan. Of course there will. Even now in the distance, above the melee, he can hear a new Christmas carol coming on as he raises his hands in the doorway, puts a new smile on his face.

"All right," Price says. "Don't worry," Price says. "Everything's all right, everything's fine. Now who wants to come see Santa? Who knows what they want?"

Miss Olive's Retreat

*Where is God? He is
where you are not —
and the Kingdom of God
is within you.*
                    — Pensées

T*he Passions of the soul,* thought Miss Olive, almost saying it
through her clenched teeth on the way back to the diner
from seeing her parents off, *disturb the senses and distort the im-
age.* Yet it took a while for even her love, Pascal, to dispel her
anger at herself. For at the last minute she had given in, back
there over the hills in the tiny airport, after letting them gab all
the way there, wear their robes of continual clamor without so
much as a nod from her. And had let down then, at the last min-
ute, there at the edge of the chain-fence boarding gate, when
they both hugged her and said, Don't you want us to say hello
from you to Aunt Ann and Uncle Elmer when we get to Sedalia?

And Miss Olive had looked at them in their cramped, careful
clothes, through their pouchy faces more familiar than her own.
Yes, she said, please do say hi. And Mr. and Mrs Olive walked
out to the plane then, waving, saying We will, we will, we will.

So now, all the way back through the green hills, the shaded
streets and skinny storefronts of Boonesboro, Pa., and the
straight long line of new road out to the old Olive Diner on the
river flat, she went over it again and again, the silent sound of the
thought like the phrases of late Beethoven she had once loved
almost as well until the silence and plan were clear and quiet
again, and the crunch of the car's tires on the gravel of the diner's
parking lot beside the weathered white frame house struck her
as sounds from someone else's world.

It was so hard, though, to make the last formal commitment,
to finally follow out her own logic; by eleven, she was over the
grill cooking up a hamburg platter for Melvie Jensen, one of the
men, half farmers, half plant workers, who lived up the side
road. He had walked in about fifteen minutes ago, while she was

foolishly checking off what food would have been needed in the next week. She shouldn't even have been there. If she'd already gone inside, he would, of course, not have been able to delay her at all.

Melvie turned on the television – too loud – at the end of the counter and sat down with his coffee across from where she stood at the grill. He acted as though he were watching the show, women talking in chairs on a flat stage, for a minute or so. Then he drummed his fingers on the table, five at a time, in some sloppy rhythm. Then laughed, as someone, too loud, was talking about what a new laundry detergent would do, incongruously, over a sink. Then talked: honest to God pleasure forgetting about the old woman, farm, things, for a few hours; glad to be out of a damn classroom for three months too if I was you; old stuff sure smells good; know it? Dull eyes floating as he mumbled, nose sniffing at the food.

When she brought it to him, he scraped the mayonnaise off his tomato. Miss Olive watched the white peel away, leaving red, and felt a vague terror. Melvie reached over, grabbed her hand with his mess of calluses, made a hopeless attempt to caress it. Know what? he said: This place'd make a goddamn fine diner. And laughed, staring hungrily up. Disgusting. She turned away, walked over to the cupboard, peeped into the cool darkness, dim objects inside. Could she find, as if by accident, Pascal there suddenly, there in the silence? Of course not. But would Pascal have a face?

Hey c'mon, Melvie said behind her, what's the trouble? When in another moment she had still not answered, she could hear his hands tearing at his napkin. The poor thing was perplexed, and with some reason. Even a year ago, it would have been at least theoretically possible for her to have let somebody like Melvie make his try, and maybe succeed. Perhaps he'd even heard from someone who had, on the spotted green couch on a summer afternoon, perhaps, while her mother napped in the house and her father worked in town on his plant shift. At that time, she'd still been backing away from the silence, seeking something randomly that could supply the same fullness. How foolish it had been, even with the gentlest, surest, driest of them. How foolish to avoid what was so clearly offered.

But she was really afraid – was she sure of what to do? Miss Olive stared at the blank plate she was washing now, water spilling over it, as though its solidity could reassure her. To be an object like the plate, to court for a while what had been stealing up on her for years. Explore, she thought, the gaps between notes. Her hand shook slightly as she placed the plate on the stack above her. She wondered too much, that was her problem; just couldn't get used to the fact that there was nothing to check back with, no perfect pitch, no correct answers in the teacher's guide to the text.

And here all these years, being plain-faced and straw-haired, her secret source of pride had been in being not so dumb. Which was almost certainly why she'd come back here to teach, she knew it, to stay a little smarter than those around her, to show a few of the smarter, more willing of them that a high school music teacher didn't have to be dumb and grossly fat. Back then she'd put more value on noise, sometimes dreamt, in fact, of young proud voices uplifted in reverential song. Bright days four years ago, cheap dreams of false beauty. The band conductor from Wilton, Leonard Samela, handsome with hooked eyebrows and a Greek face, drove to Bonesboro to talk over drinks of dual-school musical projects and the greatness of Brahms. But Samela got married, stopped coming, grew fat; the kids were monkeys in her classes, disobedient, gibbering out trivial songs (How do you solve a problem like Maria?) in bored boring voices. And this, of course, in addition to those who piled in and out of the diner every day, stupid, brutish, talking.

At first there'd only been the dim feeling that all the answers were wrong, the vague oppression of a mass of small mistakes. She slept dreadfully, drove sluggishly to school, screamed at the kids, and drove back, then washed, jerked her hair into a bun, and went next door to the diner to help with the supper crowd, and talk. She handed out plates heaped with gravy, meat, and vegetables, watched greasy mouths work, worked hers back at them as part of the service, talking about food or weather or whatever they wanted to hear, until her mouth and belly too felt full, and the place was lit with the glow of warm comfortable beasts: thank you very much, come again. Then she went back to the house, sometimes played the piano, or listened to a symphony, hated everything, went to bed with the radio on.

It got worse. She sacked the town library, blared the record player, hummed loudly, talked to anyone. In school she kept the kids singing, Little Liza Jane, Jesu Joy of Man's Desiring, it didn't matter. In the smoke-swathed faculty lounge, she invented arguments over school policy, painted spurious portraits of her students (she knew them more or less) to whoever'd listen, smoked unfamiliar cigarettes bummed from her "partners in crime" until her voice, at best coarse, got scratchy. Strangely, then she was befriended by the new girls' gym teacher, a pretty, faded wisp, Miss Rickert. One February day, after third period, she was babbling away to someone by the milk machine, and whoever she was talking to, disgusted, no doubt, walked away. She swerved this way and that, peering through the smoke for someone else to attack, and felt a small hand on her shoulder. Take it easy; I'm lonely too, said Linda Rickert, smiling, and moved off to the couch.

Miss Olive didn't follow. She stood, almost crying, wondering, Loneliness, is that what it is?

She called up Linda Rickert. They went to Tommy's, and sat in a booth drinking beer. Just like a couple of farmers, Miss Olive chirped. Miss Rickert said she was missing her friends at college, fresh out you know. Miss Olive said her friends from Mansfield State were scattered all over; she thought of them to herself, that she felt no pain at their loss. Miss Rickert shrank back in the booth, like a closing cornflower, at the sound of the men laughing, muttering, slapping each other's backs; I get enough of that at school, from the girls, she said, and giggled nervously.

They walked out into the snow. Miss Rickert began to speak, softly, earnestly, of her love, a blond bio teacher named Ricky teaching at Fort Le Boeuf outside Erie; as soon as they could find jobs that were close enough together, she said, they'd be married. She told Miss Olive she was lonely for Ricky and said, That's how come I could tell you were lonely too. Yes, said Miss Olive, It's a lonely little town all right. But even as she said it, she wondered if she and Miss Rickert were talking about the same thing. For though Miss Olive continued to talk, commiserating loudly with her new friend, she noticed the words "lonely town" did not affect her painfully, and the hushing of the snow was pleasant. Love and communication, really, that's all that's needed in the world, Miss Olive said. I couldn't agree with you more, said Miss Rickert.

Poor Miss Rickert, a patsy all the way. Miss Olive dragged her to basketball games, where she cowered and shrank as Miss Olive screeched, exhorted, booed. You must like going to these, they're right up your alley, Miss Olive brayed, and Miss Rickert, pathetically helpful, said, Sure are. Miss Olive demanded to know everything about Ricky, just everything, and wheedled until she did; then made Miss Rickert tell her again. You're the only friend I've got, she told Miss Rickert, then described to her in high rhetoric the sordid circumstances of her recent defloration and subsequent experiences with two or three men (letting on it was more) on the sofa in the back of the diner, with the TV on for sound. You are so right, she told pale Miss Rickert, Love is grand. Still frightened, Miss Rickert would not tell her to shut up, never avoided her, would not abandon her. One March night, Miss Olive asked Miss Rickert out to the house. Mr. Olive was working the four o'clock shift, Mrs. Olive was playing Five Hundred at her Card Club. Miss Olive drank enough whiskey to scare the hell out of Miss Rickert, and spoke of earthly love as the highest value of all things. Then she sat beside Miss Rickert and bent down to kiss Miss Rickert's slight, floor-burnt knees. Wispy Miss Rickert grabbed her coat, ran out the door, and submitted her resignation a week later to Principal Hanson, effective at the end of the term. She walked away quickly whenever she saw or heard Miss Olive coming down the hall waving. On the last day of school Miss Rickert's Corvair was in the parking lot, loaded, all set to leave town.

That was as bad as things got: Miss Olive was going nuts, knew it, and started to calm down. And in the very calming she found it, that will to silence. One bad day in the spring, a relapse, she caught a pugfaced monster, Litchfield, carving FART on his chair. She picked up the wastebasket, motioned the class to keep roaring, rushed up behind his intent back, and jammed the basket down over his head and shoulders. The kids stopped singing and barked laughter, the phonograph blared. Miss Olive thought of Litchfield enwrapped by the shielding metal, in the dark, perhaps soundless in there. She envied him fiercely, and jerked the basket back off.

It was, she knew, a bodying forth of what she'd been thinking through, of what had been beckoning to her all around. Months before, she'd read some Pascal in an anthology randomly snatched from the library shelves, written out passages from it on the bright yellow legal pads she bought to fill with any noisy words. She scrambled back through the pages until she found the quotes that floated dreamily in her mind: presence of a hidden God, abysses of infinity and nothing. Yes; this was it; abysses she had denied, had tried to fill with noise, music, speech, sex, like everyone else around her.

But now she knew. She read all the *Pensées,* made the kids sing, if at all, pianissimo, pretending their song issued out of all the spaces between molecules of air. By May, she merely waved them in and out of class. They were so startled by the silence that they didn't act up for a good while, only whispered, buzz buzz. With all her junior and senior high chorus practices cancelled, she sat on the bench of the Acrosonic in the living room at night, looking at the keys, often smiling. At home and school, she kept a note pad on which she occasionally printed short paragraphs, widely-spaced, to clarify her position.

Most music and speech a racket made to keep holy silence out. Exceptions Beethoven and Pascal, divide the silence into segments, without corruption, bring it closer to us. (Beethoven the deaf man, Brahms also somewhat, Pascal in the monastery). Notes, chords, words, to define the gap between them.

Holy? Who knows if God is there. But it is the reality and we won't face it, this silence, the source of the most beautiful and, not by accident, truest.

Words the original substitute for plenitude of the void. P's abysses. Any words no matter how cheap. How's the weather?

Possibility of awareness without words, like a rock. Fulfillment of stones and (perhaps) absence of color; white, emblem of purity.

Purity of act and/or perception, collects you into one mass in infinite space. P's circle of infinite circumference, whose center is everywhere.

If these keep silence between them they are all right to put down.

Miss Olive took pride in her note pad; It was indeed the best proof she had that she was progressing and could make her own formulatiȯns. And she felt no guilt for her behavior of the last year and a half, though she did wish that she had Miss Rickert's address and could write to her every now and then, just copy down some of her thoughts and send them along to let Miss Rickert see, perhaps, that she was sorry, and on the right road at last. Yet even so, there were relapses, as this morning with the folks at the airport. Or the day word finally reached the office and Principal Hanson called her in. Angular, noted for his force-fulness, he said, Some of the mothers have been told, and have told me, that there is no music in your music classes; I have checked with some of your students, and they confirm my reports.

Then he paused; Miss Olive looked up into his concerned brown eyes. Angela, he said, You've been doing a bang-up job for us for four years now, and we'd all hate to see you go. You're the best little music teacher B.H.S. ever had. He rose, walked back and forth behind the desk, eyes flashing, righteous finger pointed. Only tell me you're just tired, he said gently, That you're giving study halls because you need a rest.

Miss Olive bit her lip; her eyes watered. I'm just tired, she said, I just need a rest. It was like saying, Please do say hi for me, to her parents just now; any such lie that broke the quiet made her hate herself.

Even so, she could reason out the significance of her lapses; It was that hard to give herself wholly up. So she had plotted for herself a time when she could try without distraction. It would be now, when school was out and her parents had gone to Missouri to see some relatives, now in a prematurely hot June. Miss Olive straightened herself from her round-shouldered stoop, raised her eyes from the sink bowl, and found Melvie gone. She walked to the door and turned the sign from Olive Diner OPEN to Olive Diner CLOSED. She went out, locked the door, walked across the hot gravel to the frame house, standing unprotected in the sun; she entered the house, locked all the doors, shut all the windows upstairs and down, went to her room, shut the door, lay down on the bed, and stared up hopefully at the white plaster ceiling.

*

After a few hours, she pulls out the plug on the alarm clock. It hums very loudly, a distraction. Sweat curls and trickles onto the bedspread because air has stopped moving in the house because she has shut all the windows. With the alarm clock dead it is possible to hear the sweatdrops rolling, separate from feeling them, under the sound of her heart.

Watching the ceiling as a space unfilled is also hard. It has tiny distracting stipples that make a texture. If she allows herself to

be aware of corners, it gets hard again. Once, when she is sud-
denly able to see the ceiling as she wants to, as an absence, as a
hole, it is so frightening that she gets off the bed and leaves the
room. In the bathroom, hearing herself make a kind of music in
the bowl, she sees a razor and some bathpowder on the sink,
which she used to use: a soft past tempting with the security of
its objects. But the water is a babble rushing down and in, ugly
and painful. She gets back in the bedroom, ignoring the dresser,
the yearbooks and textbooks, the pictures of herself and Mom
and Dad, making her mind up then and there not to drink any-
thing more, not to leave the room again. She lies back down on
the bed.

She looks at the clock in the dark: no use. No cheerful orange
glow, black numbers, accurate hands, She is lying on her left
side, facing the dresser, the way her body chooses to get when
asleep, an other trick of flesh to bring her back. She straightens
out, rolls over, and looks up. On the ceiling, in the space, a let-
ter forms word by word.
Dear Miss Rickert,
Dear Mom and Dad,
Since you, like me, knew I was, have been, going through
some difficult times in the last year or so, and loved me enough
to care, I am obliged, happily, to tell you that my problems have
been self-diagnosed. I was obsessed by meaningless sound, in-
cluding most words, music, terrified by the silence, space, noise
sought to cover up. So I am now embracing, trying to embrace,
confronting, swooning into, entering –
The gap between notes; silence speech tries to make; ex-
change of self worn by words for the holy spaces, plenitude of
the void. Pascal's world and vision, Beethoven's! Can you al-
ready actually have forgotten this? But the words refuse to go up
in the space.

She wakes in snow, north sun's cold glare on everything.
Around are snowmen. They can be called names, Mom, Dad,
Miss Rickert, Samela, Hanson, melting in the sun. Carrots drop
from their heads, coal bits sink in the snow, stick arms droop
and fall under the sky.

Then it is moonless starless night – freezing hardening to crystal, stretching to every shore. Brahms and Beethoven strap on skates, glide arm in arm, their sharp steel edges cutting, patterning. Brahms' breath ices in his beard, Beethoven's black eyes gleam, as they fall to their hands and knees, try to peer down and in. Then they are gone, singing in unison. The cuts from their skates still smart.

The wrenching noise is so far beneath her she can call it by name. Phone ringing. What a joke! She can crumple up the sound, throw it away. Everything bright and holy, all that's left. Space and silence licking the wounds.

Blaise Pascal comes, skinny finger at his lips. His hair flows behind him, his black robes billow as he descends, his face is shadow-cheeked, suffused with joy. His robes enfold you as he lands, so lightly . . .

Small nasty sounds, like animals running on rocks, like cells of the body shrieking, leaving too, along with Blaise. Soured sweat or something down in your pants. Downstairs the phone rings several times. She stares up at the ceiling only because it is the least painful position for her head.

Another dirty roaring noise, louder and louder, a sforzando. There is a man standing over her, puffing and red-faced.

Holy shit, jesus jesus, he is saying, carrying her past the dresser, down the hall and stairs. Feels like you're burning right up, he is saying, kicking the screen door open, so the wind and light and color hit her like a blast. It is one of them, another of the men from up the road, she can see that now. But she cannot remember the name right now, any more than those of the road, the trees and the sun, the infinite sounds they make. This heat sure does get to you don't it? he is saying to her.

Yes, she says though it hurts her throat and only comes out in a whisper, yet it certainly will says Angela Olive trying to smile up into his face.

The Quality of Light in Maine

It was spring in the end of the sixties: Scott, Annie, and the Narrator were driving from Amherst, Mass., to Old Orchard Beach in Maine. The morning was somewhat overcast, and the towns slid by more and more sullenly – grey New England factory towns, factory removed to Hong Kong. Yet the three companions were more or less unaffected by the scenery, these possible hints of the seventies outside the car. Classes were over at our schools; we were graduating in ten days. We were playing Botticelli with the funds of knowledge we had gained. It was a G, someone in the arts. We were getting near Lowell.

"Are you the famous Spanish painter?"

Scott laughed. From the back seat it looked to the Narrator as though he drove with a little less grace than he did almost everything else; his thin shoulders hunched forward, head set straight ahead, as if locked in the effort to will the car on. "You're trying to trap me," he said. "I need more."

"Famous Spanish religious painter?"

"I'm not El Greco." His grey keen eyes never flickered. That was all the Narrator could tell in the mirror. Ahead of me Annie was tossing around in her seat; I could feel her restlessness.

"Is it a contemporary Polish playwright?" Her head jerked to the side, toward Scott. I could see the sharp lines of her profile, brow slanting to straight small nose, rounded cheeks, skin tinged with a kind of warm brown. "Five seconds," she said, raising fingers, starting to grin.

"Not Grombrowicz," Scott said.

"The eighteenth-century composer of the opera *Orfeo*?" I said.

"No," Scott said, "not Gluck."

"Are you the author of *Elective Affinities?*" I said.

"I am not Goethe."

I waited a few seconds, looked out the window. Stunted countryside, grey grass, crust of billboards over everything, the only bright colors Buy, Sell, Have A. Annie said nothing, but I could sense the spreading of her discontent; so could Scott, I thought. I waited another minute to see if he would say something to her or for her, hoping he would. We were almost to the North Shore now, and the New Hampshire line.

"Are you the famous evil conservative nineteenth-century French minister of state?"

"Under whom?"

"Louis Napoleon, I think."

Far off, the sky seemed to lighten: the ocean. The traffic grew heavier; Scott leaned forward more. "All right, you got me."

I flopped back in my seat. "Guizot. What question should I ask, Annie, what do you want to know?"

"Who cares?" she said, looking at Scott, not me, talking almost in sing-song. "Who cares about this boring game anyway? We'll never get it. You're too smart for us."

She turned her head over the seat to me and grinned wide, her face rounding and its heat moving over the seat until I was grinning too: but looking away, out the window at the Coppertone girl and dog, giant-size. "I want some dope. You want to smoke some dope, Marty?"

The billboard was past; I turned back and curled my lip at her, mock-tough. "Could be. You want to smoke, Scott?"

Scott smiled: a long mouth, fine white teeth. His eyes were still square on the road. "Good idea. Let's get stoned and listen to some groovy tunes off this here new car radio of ours."

"Some boss music," Annie said.

"Gear, man," I said.

"Right arm," somebody said, we laughed, Annie rolled the joint, we smoked it, heading north. Rain pellets struck the windshield, and Scott told us it was Fulke Greville, seventeenth-century poet complete with a sonnet cycle starting with lust for his love, ending with vows to God. He quoted us some lines, they were nice, and then we were in Maine.

The Narrator is quite stoned by the time they pull the car off the short gravel street; he is not much used to getting stoned in daylight, and their two voices from the front seat, gestures moving out of the car, lugging tote bags, seem invested with an oblique magic he does not understand. His own movements are heavy, books loose in his hands, one topples to the needle-strewn ground of the front yard: *Beethoven: His Spiritual Development*. The needles, brown, thin, half-rotten, drop from the larches nestling the darker brown-shingled cottage and dripping the morning's cold rain.

Annie and Scott were in the kitchen out back. She was putting the groceries in the fridge, on the white wooden shelves, while he bent over the old stove striking up pilot lights. I must have stood in the doorway and looked at them, stoned, arms full of books and my decrepit gym bag, for a full minute.

"Just dump your stuff," she said, and I spilled it over the yellow linoleum table where their bags sat. "We've got to get this place cleaned and opened up before anything else." She liked giving orders; they gave her voice a hard but not unpleasant edge, her mouth and brow a small scowl. "There's a broom by the back door. You can take it and sweep the needles off the porch while you" – her eyes flicked Scott leaning against the stove – "start the pump."

Then he is alone again: the Narrator, narrating to himself. His feet in moccasins pad over the needles, the grey chipping paint of the porch. Between the broom's scratches he can hear the soft sound of the water still falling from the trees on the porch roof and, more crisply, on the ground outside. He can hear soft talk of birds in the woods across the street, a film of full green through the screens. He is still stoned enough to wonder how the needles, so many of them, get through; then he sees the slit, perhaps two inches high, that runs from beam to beam around the porch. Air moves cool across his fingers when he puts his hand down: for extra coolness in the summertime? He tries to place a set of parents, Scott's, whom he has never met, upon the red porch swing. It is a humid night in July, bugs tap the screens. Scott, his face already complete, carved out, plays on the floor: a game of chess. Birds shout from the woods. He places Scott and Annie on the swing, slowly rocking. What are they talking about, are they kissing, do they kiss with any heat? Annie stands before him in the kitchen, between him and the refrigerator, with a Gioconda smile: she crosses her arms around her waist, brown arms, and lifts and peels the black turtleneck off: her round breasts appear, move toward him. Off in the woods the birds coo. He is very happy; here, at this time of his life in Maine, in this house of Scott's unknown family, with Annie and Scott, life seems to have the potential to be a work of art.

Minneapolis, in the seventies, a hot day in June. Scott and Annie's apartment is so near the Pillsbury plant that the air on the street outside clouds with the sweet, choking scent of grains, a smell of glut. We walk down the sidewalk, shrouded by elms, and Annie talks.

"I met him through some friends, people I have class with at the university. There was a party, Scott didn't want to go – no, he had to work that night, that's right."

She pauses; and I am aware of her masked face under the speckles of sweet green light, held still as a small hunting or hunted animal's. I think: she has caught herself trying to blame Scott.

She smiles and tosses her head; her eyes glance to the side at me. "I danced with him a few times, talked to him some, even met his wife at one point. He told me about his life. It was an amazing story. Do you know he started out with nothing? His parents are dirt farmers in Oklahoma. He ran away when he was sixteen with this woman he married, and went to L.A. to learn film."

"No," I say, with a smile I hope shows precise amounts of sympathy and ironic wisdom. "No, I don't know that." Then, with apparent casualness, watching her closely: "Do you love him?"

She frowns; her brown eyes flatten and lose their light, as though struggling over a sum. "Maybe I do." Then she grabs my bare arm and, while the shudder thrills up it, down my back, sending my gaze away from her face down to her leather sandals: "Oh Marty, *you* know what it's like when it starts, though, the way you want to be in bed with them all the time and talk and eat with them and you can't get them out of your head. Is that love? I don't know. But that's how it is."

"I don't know either," I say, "but I know what you mean." And so I do, but not so well or often as she thinks. I understand her fantasies of me as Don Juan, her fictions on the subject of my life in California, when I am not with them: the life a part of herself would have. My own opinion of my few affairs is that they are modest, scrupulously limited, and a little tired; though there are many reasons why I would just as soon Annie never found that opinion out. "How is Scott taking all this?" I say.

We have broken out into a sunlight so dense it dulls the green of the park to our left and burns my eyes. "Scott," she says, as if his name were itself a statement, and turns and plops down on the browning grass. Against the ground and in this light, the blacks, blues, purples of her batiked shift smear further and seem to bleed her back into the lawn. "Well, he's doing just what you'd expect. When I told him about it, he cried a little but not for very long. Then he asked me if I wanted a divorce."

"Do you?" I say, easing down next to her. Already sweat sticks my white T-shirt to my back, lies on my arms and hands like a thin paste.

"No," she says and bites her lip before starting again. "Anyway, he told me that he loved me. And that if this was what I wanted, he wants it for me too. And now he's just the same" – she turns her head to me, her open, hungry face – "I mean, you've been with him the last few days, isn't he just the same?"

I try to see through the heat Scott's face during the last two days of my visit, his movements through the shady apartment, his talk. "I don't know," I say, watching my hands grope to say it for me, "maybe I'm projecting. But when I think about it, he doesn't seem to" – the fingers try to shape something, I smile lamely – "well, *move* the same way. I mean, he leans back into chairs, he talks slower. The other day, he was telling me something about Pound, what it was like reading the *Cantos* –"

"Oh yeah, Pound," she says tonelessly, her face hidden downward.

"Yeah, right," I say; but the image of the lean face startled, haggard, figure sagged into the beanbag chair, hands fumbling like mine now is too strong. "Still, the thing is, it was like he forgot what he was saying, he had put it on automatic pilot without even knowing it and it ran out on him. And I've never seen Scott at a loss before."

Even through the heat, we both can feel the same image of him hanging, floating: Scott, different from us. Scott like a deer.

Then Annie looks earthward again. "Sometimes, even when we were first going together I used to think, 'He's so smart but he doesn't know anything. Nothing's ever happened to him.'" Out of the corner of my eye, like a distortion from the heat, I can see the twist of her mouth. "Well, now something has, but he doesn't want to admit it. Doesn't want to admit he's mad or he wants me, or it hurts him, doesn't want to fight for me at all, no, he's too good for that. Then, when we do sleep together?"

She hesitates; does she want to tell me this, is she a bitch? And me, do I want to see it, her rich body listless on the sheets, some shame spreading from him, old lust fogging my eyes like heat? "Yes?" I say. "Yes, what?"

Her fingers make claws held out in the sun. "He clutches. The way he clutches and holds on so to me."

Then her face is turned up and open, sweat dotting her forehead too, set lips like rage, sun glaring the face as bright as in my sweaty dreams and "You know me," she is saying almost fiercely, "you and I, we know each other, we're alike, that's why I love you so much. You know he *has* to be mad somewhere, but he won't show it. Tell him he is. Get it out of him. It can't go on like this, he's got to get it out."

Her hot eyes close to mine as any lover's, the sick scent of the grain as if from her breath on my face, and sweat breaking finally down my brow and cheeks: "Okay," I say, "I'll try. If you think it'll do him some good."

"So do you," she whispers, almost hissing.

"Yeah, right," I say, getting up. "So do I."

On the way back to the apartment, then, we talk about our fathers; hers still scratching out a living on a Pennsylvania farm, mine still trying to be happy as a foreman at the tire plant back in Akron. We laugh at and feel miserable about them at the same time, and for a moment neither one of us is thinking about Scott. She's right, of course; we are alike. But even in the shade now, the heat seems unbearable.

They walk, the three of them, through the town of Old Orchard, two blocks on their way to the beach, deserted as a stage set. A stage set, thinks the Narrator, passing the brown little bank, church of weathered white clapboards, neat green of the tiny square: as if there were nothing behind these fronts so clean in their particularity, as if you could poke though them, push them over. But he is too stoned to understand this as a function of the quality of light in Maine; and besides, Scott is pointing and talking, his face stamped out clean against the sky. "Here's where I work in the summer," he says, waving his hand to the left.

I look at the stores, the green, the two tennis courts, the flagpole. "Where?"

"The courts," Annie says softly, and winds her arm around Scott's waist. "Scott's the Old Orchard tennis pro, gives lessons and everything."

"Slight misrepresentation," he says, grinning at both of us. "This was back in high school. And I had to sweep the courts down after rain and mend the nets. You don't have to be Rod Laver to be the Old Orchard tennis pro."

A few steps more and the giggles rise like someone else's pumped into my mouth. They start to laugh too. "What's funny?" one of them says.

"A minute ago, when you said there's where you worked?" I say, gasping it out. "I was looking around the place, looking for where it could be. I was looking for some kind of plant." And they both laugh harder too.

Then the sidewalk becomes planks set in the dunes and they run out and we are on the beach for the first time. The sky is still overcast and it is cold. The goddamn Atlantic Ocean, thinks the Narrator, it really is slate-grey. While he has been watching it, the other two have moved, farther down, and now he turns to watch them: the young man in his orange trunks, woman in her lime two-piece. They are settling their blanket. They are putting their books, their radio on it. They are holding and kissing each other against the sky while gulls wheel overhead, everything in a tight, perfect composition of Lovers, Sea, Sky he will not disturb until it breaks, they break apart. Then he goes running over the beach to them without taking off his sneakers, so that they fill up quickly with gritty wet sand.

"You know what?" he says when he gets there. "This goddamn sea really is slate-grey. This is the slate-grey sea."

"Klutz," Annie says, scowling, shaking her head. "You got sand all over the blanket, good Christ."

"But it is also," Scott says, lifting a finger, "wine-dark."

"And froth-chained," I say, pointing back.

"Yet leaden," he says with long horsey face.

"Incessant," I say, "yet somehow – imperturbable."

Annie is belly down on the blanket already, her halter strap unhitched, the radio on. "Primeval," she mutters. "The cradle of life. Why don't you two hacks run along? Go swimming, see if that gives you any new cliches."

The Narrator watches Scott bend down and move his hand over Annie's bare brown back. The Narrator notes that the hair of Scott's head and body, quivering slightly in the breeze, is the same color as the sand. "Warm down here," Scott says, "you're under the wind." The Narrator watches Annie stir under Scott's hand. "Yes," Annie says. "Don't fall asleep or forget to roll over," Scott says. "Cloudy days up here, people get burned before they know it." "I know," she says. "I've sunbathed before, I'll be fine."

Scott rises. As a backdrop, behind the faunlike face, the Narrator finds a chain of cliffs stretching off to the south. And the quality of light in Maine is such that their distance from him makes itself known only by spatial perspective; for the jagged shape of the farthest cliff stands as clear as the one that is only a hundred yards away.

When Scott gets off his shift I pick him up at the hospital and take him to a bar. While I ply him first with pitchers of beer, then with manhatttans, Irish whiskey, Old Grandads to crack him apart, he sits across a wooden table still in his orderly's smock, and tells me funny stories about his work.

"Then there's Callahan, another old-timer," he says, eyes gleaming, head starting to weave. "The nurses told me he was crazy, you had to watch for him. Nobody ever knew what he was talking about. I couldn't either at first, but I liked it. He spun out these strings of incredible images, one after another, and they didn't make the least bit of rational, linear sense. Then" – he opens his hands on the table, leans forward his thin, smiling face – "I realized that he was talking poetry. He had gotten tired of ordinary discourse, he made metaphor instead. When he was going to get a barium treatment, he'd say he wanted a pearl-handled revolver with a silver bullet in it, he was going to shoot his stomach from his mouth. See what I mean?"

Then again, the moment: his eyes flee mine, he looks up as if someone had called to him and his face collapses into shadows. It is just a second, but enough; it is time now. "Let me think," he says, "what were some of the other ones?"

I raise a hand from the table and prop my forehead with it and make myself look straight at him. "Annie told me today she has a lover."

He smiles in a thin-lipped way that, in my own drunkenness perhaps, could be almost, almost taken as snide; then it breaks genuine, generous, soft. "Yes, I know," he says.

"I know you do," I say. "She told me that too." And now I have my arms out on the table, palms up, and am leaning toward the floating wooden face, darkened eyes. "Scott," I say, "I'm not trying to hurt you or taunt you or anything. I just want to know what you're doing about it and how you feel."

The caving in of his cheeks, twist in his lips are definite now; though I am too drunk to know exactly how it makes me feel. Now it's going to come out, I think, he'll purge himself. And also I think: you dirty shithead, you're hunting the deer.

"I'm doing nothing about it," he says very neutrally. "I want her to be able to do anything she wants. What she wants right now makes me sad. I don't feel very good about it. But it's what she wants to do. And besides," he says with the same lack of any tone, "I still have a decent life. The job is all right, I only have a year to go before the C-O's done and I can go back to school. I have my books, I even have Annie most of the time, you know. She still spends more time with me than with him."

This last without the slightest trace of pride or boastfulness; without the slightest trace of anything. He picks up his glass and drinks from it as if washing down his throat after a speech delivered too many times. Just to Annie, or himself too? I wonder, and cannot find the end of the thought for the rush of feelings in me, the same she must have when he tells her the same damn thing. "Goddamn it, Scott," I say, bringing my fist down on the table, grateful for the cover of the alcohol, "but goddamn it, don't you ever get mad? Don't you ever want to kick the guy's face in? Or hers?"

He smiles; a smile that turns his face radiant, as if with gentle victory. "I'll tell you something that may sound silly to you, but it's true. When I was very small – eight, maybe – I decided I was never going be be angry again. Anger never seemed to solve anything, I could never control it, and it was unpleasant. Then, later, I thought of another reason; people should always be able to do what they want, especially the people you love." He stood up then, his white coat bright and clean in the bar's dark, like a cassock, like an icon of some damn saint. "Now maybe we better go home," he said, smiling. "I've got to work tomorrow. Here, let me help you pay for some of this."

But by the time we are in the car and on our way home, my mind is flooded again with an image too much stronger than his thin, studied composure, his smile in the bar and now; the picture of him covered with sweat and tears, clinging to Annie's body in the middle of these humid Minnesota nights.

The Narrator is in Maine, seated on one end of an old leather couch, its brown slick surface webbed with tiny cracks. The Narrator is reading *Beethoven: His Spiritual Development* by J.W.N. Sullivan, the chapter on Art and Reality. He reads: "It is characteristic of the greatest art that the attitude it communicates to us is felt by us to be valid, to be the reaction to more subtle and comprehensive contact with reality that we can normally make." He has read this sentence three times slowly, trying to decide if it is stupid or if it makes a sense beyond what he can know. But he cannot decide.

He looks up. Though it is night and the lamps glow orange off the pine walls, there is still an almost crystal quality about the scene: Annie curled up at the other end of the couch, frowning over *Washington Square*, Scott in the stuffed chair across from him focused effortlessly on Wallace Stevens. "Stop," the Narrator says.

They look up, their reading expressions still on. "What's the last sentence you read?"

Scott says: "The ever-hooded, tragic-gestured sea was merely the place by which she chose to sing."

Annie says: "Love demands certain things as a right; but Catherine had no sense of her rights; she had only a consciousness of immense and unexpected favors." She fidgets and frowns. "My back is driving me crazy. Will you rub some Noxema on it for me?"

"Sure," I say.

When she is down on the brown and green braided rug, in sunbathing position, blue blouse rolled up over the slightly pink skin, and I am astraddle her ass, dipping fingers into the cool white paste, Scott looks up from his book again and says: "Why'd you ask?"

Off the fingers, onto the firm flesh, the paste warms, becomes cream. "Ahhh," Annie sighs; it is hard to be the Narrator, detach myself from this warmth, rubbing, watch her and answer Scott myself at the same time. "I don't know," I say as the Narrator smooths over the rise of scapulae, softness at the edge of the shoulder, reddening brown. "I was reading this sentence about art, what it can do, and thinking about all of us sitting around reading art. And I wondered" – rubbing the sheen into the flesh until it disappears, she keeps moaning softly Oh that's good, the Narrator listens to her – "I've had this funny sense ever since we got here, and maybe before, ever since, you know, we've been friends" – feeling silly saying it, while the Narrator watches the fingers stroke the slippery ridge of spine, pressing for the bone Oh that's nice please don't stop – "that everything's fitted together in some very clean way, if you can just see it that way. So the thing about the quotes just now was a kind of a test."

"God, that's wonderful," Annie murmurs. "You've got a genius pair of hands." The Narrator watches hands move in wide circles, press the hot skin.

"And did they fit with your quote?" Scott says.

"I'm not sure. Maybe so. And remember anyway, I said if you can see it that way."

"And even if you could," Scott says, smiling slightly, enjoying himself, "who could tell if that was art or life?"

The Narrator stopped moving, stopped watching; I looked very closely at Scott. "Which is it for you?"

"Either," he said, grinning wide and friendly. "Both. I'm reading Wallace Stevens."

"Stop talking," Annie said. "Frost said Stevens wrote on bric-a-brac and Frost was right. All just surfaces. Rub me."

And I did. I rubbed cool cream into her broad firm back until I could no longer be the Narrator watching it or even fully myself, even the weightless ache of my loins somewhere behind, all that was happening that melting touch of hands and skin, that smooth slick pressure. While Scott read on in his Wallace Stevens the only sound was from her an occasional murmur of groan, the light thickened to golden heat, until I was rubbing the very skin off her back in tiny curds my motion rolled into small balls on her smooth back when she said: "Oh, that was so nice. I know I'll sleep just great now. Coming, Scott?"

It was hard to remember that moment clearly, or to fit it in later on, while I took off my clothes in Scott's brother's room upstairs, where the wood was darker and the air was cool. On a shelf across from the bed were swimming ribbons, tennis awards, and some books: *Lost Horizon, The Yearling, Wild Ani-*

mals I Have Known. There were no pictures of the boy; so it was easy for me to imagine, for a long moment on the edge of sleep, growing up myself that way, the way of Scott and Scott's bother, summering in Maine and learning tennis and swimming and reading the right books for an thirteen year old, learning a life as clean and cool, as composed as the air and light in Maine: being Scott's brother. As I thought of these things, my groin stopped aching, and I fell asleep.

*

After that visit, I went back to California; but Scott and I kept in touch with letters. His told me of his reading, the weather, his job, with an occasional reference to Annie and her lover, who were fine. For a while, the three of them moved into a house together, close by the river, with a beautiful view, Scott said.

But when the C-O ended, Scott wrote to say the two of them had said goodbye to the film editor and were moving to Cambridge, where he'd been accepted into Harvard's Ph.D program; again, I could detect no malice or triumph between the lines. After that, our letters passed less frequently. His became less witty and less careful, trains of mild observations on classes and books. I wondered what psychic price he had to pay to win Annie back with exemplary behavior, and what price she had had to pay to lose. But she never wrote.

Six months ago I saw them again. I had finally got an agent, the agent had sold a story, and Scott had just accepted a job offer from Wesleyan; when I scraped up enough money to go see my agent in the flesh, we made plans to meet in New York. They knew a little bar, thought it was still there, in the East Village . . .

New York jars me. Downtown, near my agent's office, there are too many people with too much money, dressed like the ads in the *Times* Sunday Magazine and moving very quickly to get more, stay ahead, not get caught up in the random movements of the shabby desperadoes and wrecks they share the sidewalks with. My agent spoke despairingly of my lack of commercial sense; I was writing about the wrong people, she said. What with all this, the pigeons screaming doomed traffic reports, and a grey drizzle in the air, I knew I would not be seeing Scott and Annie with a very clear head. Besides, I had given up being a Narrator as a bad habit long ago.

The bar was tubular chrome, red vinyl, junior executive types, male and female, loudly displaying their charms. Scott and Annie have to come up and tap my arm. "Marty."

I turn and hug them before looking. Scott's body is still lean. Annie's feels softer, rounder; I feel no ache.

"Let's go sit down," Scott says turning away. "Then you tell us how you broke into the Big Apple today."

While I make a story out of my agent's dire innuendoes, I look them over. My sense of touch was correct. Scott has grown a full, sandy moustache, though, and his face is narrower than ever; almost a ferret's now. And though Annie's figure in the green caftan does seem fleshed out, her brown eyes are harder than I remembered them. Then again, though, maybe it's just this place. "But you're the ones who've made it," I say as soon as I can. "What's with you? Tell me about the job."

"It's two classes a semester," Scott says while Annie leans forward, watching, stroking her glass. "One Freshman Comp, one Survey English Lit, one Victorian Novel, and a graduate seminar in Victorian Studies."

"It's a beautiful job," Annie says, looking straight at me. "Nobody gets English jobs like this one any more. Four classes a year and tenure-track."

Scott glances at her and starts a smile that wavers on his face. His eyes seem to lose their focus. "That's great," I say. "And your dissertation's in?"

His eyes snap back, but not quite; as if they look only inward, into himself. "And approved," he says and starts to pick with one hand at the cuff of his powder-grey suit. "But there's still something I don't like about it. It's not clear enough, it doesn't say exactly what I mean. What I was trying to do is make a case for a non-dramatic reading of Ruskin's aesthetics." He keeps on picking at the imaginary lint, he is not looking at me any more, and his words are coming rather fast. "You see, the way I think Ruskin must be read is with all his historicizing stripped away, the story element and all the bombast peeled off, and only then can we see the clear, simple airy structure of the aesthetic itself. See Marty," he says, "*I* think –"

"It's a great dissertation," Annie says and backs fingers through her brown shagged hair. "His judges all told him it was publishable. One of Scott's professors has already sent it on to a press, with his recommendation attached."

"I'm sure it's all right," I say. "Scott, you've always been able to say exactly what you mean."

Scott smiles out of the side of his mouth. Annie fiddles with her glass, I chew my cherry. Nothing seems really terribly wrong. "So," I say, "when are you moving?"

"Next month," says Annie, with a trace of her old frown. "We're getting a place in a new development on the edge of town. It's two-story, brick, sort of colonial, right up next to the woods. We'll lease with an option to buy. You'll really have to come and see us more often, now that we're finally going to be in one place."

I picture the house a moment – almost like the old Narrator – then delete it. "That'd be nice," I say, "I'll try. But I really don't have much more money than I ever did."

"Why do you live in California anyway?" Scott says, tipping his head and leaning close to me, breathing a bitter smell. His stomach must be eating him alive. "We miss you, old friend. Why don't you come up to Cambridge right now and spend a few days?"

"I can't," I say. "I'd love to but I can't. The money's too tight. I have to be back day after tomorrow punching the clock at Ray-Chem in Redwood City, CA."

Scott's mouth twists in a funny way, a way I have never seen before. "You can get jobs like that here too that'll keep you in touch with those people you write about," he says.

Those people. I think about what my agent has just told me; about the people I work with; the people I have lived with since I was born, except for my college days. "Those people," I say, looking back at him as neutrally as I can.

Scott rubs his nose and looks down at the table. "Well, we do miss you, don't we Annie?" he says, and pats her hand.

"Yes," she says, staring hard at me, "we do."

A minute later he excuses himself to go to the bathroom and I am left alone with Annie, still watching me sullenly. Her face *is* rounder, fuller though –

"Hey," I say suddenly, lunging forward in the chair, "are you pregnant?"

She smiles politely, reaches for her drink. "About three months," she says. "How'd you know?"

"Just something about you," I say; and can't help smiling. "You look filled out. But how do you feel about it? Are you glad?"

"It was planned," she says. "I'm glad."

"You two must be happy together then," I say.

She shrugs. "I suppose."

It makes me mad. She's pushed him, I think, she's molded him, she has kept him as her lover all along and she doesn't have the decency to be pleased. "Listen," I say, keeping my face quite still. "Did you get what you wanted from him out of that affair? Are you satisfied now?"

Her eyes narrow, lips press tight. "I don't know what you mean," she says and turns, and almost whispers. "Here he comes."

I turn my head too, and watch him moving through the thick expensive crowd, his gaze directed myopically to the match and bowl of his briar pipe. He lights and puffs blue clouds of smoke: a few other people look on after him; and I watch Annie watching him with her own sour, defeated face.

The rest of the time we spent in Maine passed in the way I have described to you. But there is one incident I remember out of that time that stays so sharply in my mind that I am not sure if it happened or if I dreamed it. And if I dreamed, whether I dreamed it then or later on.

It is very simple, really. I was walking along the edge of the deserted beach at Old Orchard, close to the dunes. A crisp steady wind blew into me, filling my ears with a low roar. I passed a pocket in the sand dunes, and knew Scott and Annie were there. I turned and walked up into the dunes, at the edge of the pocket; and there they were, lying together on a bright striped towel. They lay on their bellies, completely still; he in his orange trunks, she in her lime two-piece, their beautiful faces close together, completely still, completely clear. The two of them together filled the space that framed them; and the quality of light in Maine that makes the surfaces of things so clean and complete, illumined them completely and made them both, on that towel and in that pocket of sand, a work of art.

I have walked into a work of art, I thought; and the thought both thrilled and frightened me so much that I stepped out of the dunes and turned back up the beach. But when I repassed that pocket they were awake, alive, standing up. Annie beating the sand off the towel with hard, slapping motions, her face swollen and angry; Scott squinting vaguely off at the darkening sky; the wind gone and, ahead of me, light falling dully on the sand that stretched off into haze.

The Collected Works of Brown

*Brown, Theodore Anselm: Born near Boonesboro, Pa.,
July 7, 1899, son of Thomas and Hedwig Brown. Served
during World War I with the 142nd Regiment of the
United States Army. Married Virginia Fannocks, also
of Boonesboro. Employed by the Wespenn Manufactur-
ing Company from 1920 to 1965 as a maintenance
man. Member of the Calvary Lutheran Church. Pres-
ently surviving relatives a sister, Anna Shrifton of
Scranton, Pa., and several nieces and nephews. Cur-
rently in residence at 524 Main St., Boonesboro, Pa.*

You mop too wet and they just come in before it's dry and
track black all over the place, especially all round the johns,
and you just have to wipe up all over again.

*

One summer day when he was six, he had just finished sweep-
ing out the barn when his older brother Curt called him to come
up on the hill and play Indians. But as they went, Curt walked
faster and faster up the hill and wouldn't wait for him to catch
up. Finally Curt ran away from him and disappeared into the
blackberry bushes which grew all over the path.

He called for Curt, but there was no answer. He was left
alone. So he sat down on a large round rock beside the path to
catch his breath before going back down the hill. But the sun
was very hot, a heavy sweet smell rose from the bushes, and the
hum of many insects reached his ears. He lay down on the stone
and began to go to sleep.

As his sleep became deeper and deeper, a sound in the woods
got louder and louder, the sound of a saw on a tree. He heard
this sound in his sleep and dreamed he was at a table where a
giant sat eating and growling. When the tree fell he woke up and
was so confused he thought for a minute there really was a giant
chasing him to eat him. So he ran down the hill and out of the
woods as fast as he could. And even though he realized after a
while that it wasn't a giant, he was still scared for a long time,
even after his father told him it was only the jacks cutting timber

on the back hill past the farm.

*

Talk to me, the army nurse said.

She came in every day and stood before him with the same starched smile. His distaste for her jolly, uniformed self and mission had deepened until it became the strongest emotion Ted felt. She jarred him more and more, not back to himself, but forward to the vague, disturbing, angry feelings he felt draping over him sometimes at night.

He turned his head from her official happiness, wincing from the pain that jumped from his bandaged leg and neck, and stared out at the hospital garden. It was still raining. Pools covered the black soil that had drifted under his fingernails and into his face on march. Tulips drooped, their colors fading, beaten down by the rain that had glutted them.

How do you expect to learn to talk again if you don't try? she said.

Get out, Ted said suddenly, clearly. But then his head lapsed back again against the pillow.

*

There's the things you have to do, sure, but you can always pick the order you're gonna do them in. It's good too to make yourself out a list. That way you can look there on the inside of your locker when you get there in the morning and see it all up there printed out for yourself. There's other stuff too, you know, like not ripping the wrapping off the shitpaper til the dispenser's unlocked, and that stuff you just learn when you've been here for a while. And when you get tired and you got your work done for a while just go to a stall and drop drawers and sit there, you know, so nobody finds you. That stuff, though, that's just tricks of the trade you learn for yourself. They come natural.

*

Brown found no hidden beauty in Virginia Fannock's faded, square body; Virginia never thrilled to hear his limping step on the porch of her parents' house. And yet their marriage, when it came, was not merely one of convenience. They did drift together, into wordless, passive coupling; each had sensed from the start that the other had little chance somehow of marrying anyone else. Yet under their coldness, loneliness, their fear of isolation, lay a separate, positive hope. Each wanted to see and so, eventually, saw in the other's very separateness, the other's life, the possibility of finding rest in some unknown absolute, of breaking through somehow. What absolute, what to break through? They could not have said; they had no words; they were barely conscious of the hope. So, with little conversation and less lovemaking, in dread of their own desires, they were married after a long courtship, in 1921.

*

On the boat to France, the men around him seemed to talk about it all the time. They rested their arms on the rail and peered out anxiously at the horizon; but their voices were strangely hushed and calm.

Yeah, there was one I knew in Portland. Francine. No whore either but she sure . . .

So we got off and walked into the orchard. That was the best damn . . .

Ted heard them as he passed along the deck. The image rose to his mind of the boy's body hulked over his sister's, crushing her into the wet earth. His stomach sickened and the breath tasted sour in his mouth. He went back to his bunk and lay down. But even then the stories still reached him, murmured by disembodied voices in other bunks.

After a while they had their effect. He began by running over them unconsciously, like prayers, at the end of each day. They came to fascinate him, they were like magic. Waves of sad beauty washed from them and fell against his heart.

Two weeks before he was wounded, he finally got laid by a girl who worked at one of the bars in the French town where he was billeted. It was over quickly; afterwards, he remembered no beauty, but was able to feel a pleasant, hazy melancholy until he recalled that the tables in the front of the bar had given off a scent of spoiled wine, and that he was out some money.

*

Some of the guys, they'll play jokes like the time they threw the firecracker over the stall door and he thought he was going to have his blown off before he could get his pants up, and they kid you a lot about sitting on the john for a living and all, but you just wait and listen to them when there's nothing for them to wipe their ass with or no soap or clean towels, they know what you're there for then by God. It's not all that soft to keep a good place for them to come clean up when they come in and out with all that sweat and dirt, don't even look half the time to see if they hit where they're aiming so after every one you have to get the joni mop back out and wipe the urinal down before you can sit back down again. Oh, they're a rough crew all right, but they aren't so bad.

*

His mother was prettier than anybody. She shelled peas on the porch with his father beside her. He, Teddy, was sitting on the edge of the porch with Anna and Petey. Neighbors said Anna took after his mother. But Anna was ugly and had brown hair, not yellow and grey.

Curt was in the barn doing chores. It was getting dark out. The peas went plop in the pot at his mother's feet.

Look up there, his father said, and pointed at the hill.

What? Anna said.

He couldn't see what either. His father went into the house for the rifle, and sat in the porch rocker to fire it. Then his father pulled his rope out of his pocket, ran across the yard, and up the hill.

What is it? Anna said, but his mother didn't answer. There was a ringing in his ears from the gun. Plop went the peas in the pot.

Shut up, Anna, Petey said.

Don't talk that way to your sister, his mother said.

His father had shot a deer, a big buck, and dragged it down to the house, then sat down hard, all out of breath on the porch beside him. Hot damn, his father said, all sweating, and some blood on his hands, That's as good a shot as I ever made.

We don't need any meat now Tom, his mother said. Not with that pig fresh killed.

Plop, plop, plop, went the peas.

What'd you shoot at? yelled Curt, coming up from the barn. The deer's tongue was out of its mouth against the grass.

*

Inevitably, after the first few months of married life, both found themselves disappointed, as their days were marked by bitter quarrels, real shouts and tears. Yet even this violence was tempered by their fear. Deliberately ignorant of their loss, their failure, they could only fight over trivia – household chores, when Brown should get home from work, whether or not they should buy a new broom, or a radio. And even had they known what had been lost (that absolute, that vague escape which perhaps never could be found), or had language to speak of it, still it would probably never have been mentioned. To do so would have been risking desolation. Soon their voices faltered before they were raised; eventually they lacked any force at all. Finally their grievance became unfelt; they bought an expensive radio, and played it all day.

*

So they all went to the little school each day, Curt and Petey and he and Anna. The school was a long ways away, and they had to walk to it, lots of times in very bad weather. It was a very small wooden school. He sat next to Petey in the middle of the room; Curt and Anna were at the sides because they were older. Sometimes Petey pestered him.

Miss Gudgeon said, You students absolutely must be quiet while I am teaching another grade. We cannot do with noise in this room.

She had a mole on her lip. He watched it and was quiet.

Petey tickled him one day and wouldn't stop. So he tried to watch the mole so he wouldn't laugh. It had tiny black hairs growing out of it. He squinted to see them so he would not laugh. He laughed and Miss Gudgeon hit him across the face and smacked up Petey too. He saw Anna watching with very black eyes.

*

Every so often, especially after Ginnie was gone and on days when the arthritis and poor circulation in his leg were acting up, Ted woke with a tremendous hankering to go back to the plant and see how things were going.

One day he was sitting in the recliner watching tv, trying to decide again whether he should go or not, when the pain in his leg started edging up his side in spurts, sharp in a way he could hardly remember pain ever to have been. When he was sure he was going to die, he grabbed his coat and left as fast as he could, before it was too late.

Once he had passed the factory gateman and was inside the plant, he wondered what to do next. Some of the men at the furnaces and belts waved to him and shouted his name. He lurched past them into the john. Immediately the pain became softer, almost caressing, as he moved toward the third stall where he had spent so much of his time. Sitting there was a release, too; automatically his bowels began to churn. Men shuffled in the john as he sat; he could still remember the routine well enough to know still who it was who had his break just then and used it to piss. Three times he was able to recognize a man by the sound of his step.

When, after a long while, a mop flicked under the stall door, Ted wiped himself, flushed hurriedly, and walked out to meet the new janitor. He was a young guy with brown hair and glasses, and he was mopping too wet. Ted introduced himself and they shook hands. The new man was something like he had been, not very talkative on the job; he kept on mopping, making little puddles all over the floor, pressing down too hard on a mop that was too wet.

You know, Ted said, I believe you might just be mopping a little too wet. See, when the guys come in now, they'll –

Hey, do you think I give a sweet shit? the new man said.

Ted's eyes began to water. He jerked backward, and grabbed for the door. Well, it's all yours now, he said.

The new man smirked. Yeah, he said.

When Ted opened the front door of his house, he was met by a burst of applause. The television set was still on. He turned it off and went straight to bed although it was only around eleven o'clock in the morning.

*

To change the Roll-A-Towel, you just open up the casing and wind the rest of the towel on the lower roller. Then you take the lower roller off with the towel around it and put the upper roller in for the lower roller and take the one with the towel to supply and get a fresh one from them all rolled up but without a roller. So you take the roller out of the center of the dirty one and shove it in the center of the clean one. This you take back to the john and put in for the upper roller and unroll part of the towel, enough to go around the casing where it hangs down and get to the lower roller or maybe a little more, and you wind it around the lower roller until it won't unroll from the lower roller by itself, then just put the casing back up.

*

Ted kept running through the trees because it was impossible to stand still. Occasionally the woods came to an end and he found himself in a field. Even though the woods were being torn apart by the shelling, he was more afraid of the fields. They banked irregularly in gullies, crossing and recrossing each other. Each time he ran into a dip, he saw a picture of the grinning machine-gunner that would be there, or the black mine. The sky was broken with clouds he could see whenever the shelling stopped. At first the shelling had been very loud in his ears, and distinct from the other noises of machine guns, rifles, and mines; then he could even hear his boots crunch leaves and break twigs in the woods. But the noises all ran together now and howled in his head like a long train passing very near.

He tripped and fell on the edge of a hole. As he picked himself up, someone ran past him screaming Come on, goddammit, come on! We're past the machine gunners!

The notion that the machine gunners were behind him somewhere struck him as funny; he pictured them with tough shaved heads, firing at trees and ground. His own rifle smacked against his hip; it was a stupid hunk of wood and metal, stupid and clumsy. He let it slip off his shoulder as he entered the next patch of woods.

He was so tired he was trotting hunched over when the falling tree limb hit him above the ankle of his right leg. The limb was too heavy to lift off, but the pain soon was as dull as the noise. The limb curved around so its tip was near his face; it still had some leaves on it. He contented himself with looking at the veins running along a dry orange leaf and tracing them with his fingers until the shell hit near him and a fragment lodged in his throat. Then all the color drained out of everything very quickly, and he wondered just before he shut his eyes if he was hurt so badly that nothing would ever have color or sound right again. Still, he was pretty sure he wasn't going to die.

*

To come home from work after nineteen years and find Virginia sobbing red-faced on the couch filled Brown with anger and fear. Her tears were transgressions, risking everything they had. Reopening now was the void they had patched over so painstakingly a long, long time ago.

What's the matter with you now? he said.

Nothing.

Well, if you're going to your woman's thing there at church tonight you'd better straighten up, he said, only a little more softly: Look a mess if you don't.

But she persisted, whimpering through supper, staying in afterwards to snuffle in the living room, avoiding his eyes, while his jangling senses jumped back at him, making the meatloaf sharp to his tongue, the radio harsh in his ears. It was as if she were threatening him with that open grief. She seemed obscene, obscene and frightening, as if he had been forced out of himself by her, and into a nightmare of dread.

Finally, in bed, even his silence fell away; he grabbed her shoulders and demanded she comply and shut up.

And Virginia was glad to tell him; she too was full of the same dread. Went to the doctor today, she said, snuffling: He says there's probably no chance we can have kids any more. Says I'm too old now.

As the words reached the air, they seemed to deaden; both Brown and Virginia felt an inestimable sense of relief. The words gave a reason: a reason meant that they could push their anguish away. Virginia's agony flowed back down the hole from which it had gushed, in the image of the child she would never have; while Brown's horror spread itself thin between a feeling of surprise that all this trouble had, after all, followed out of the very habit of caution, and the idea, faintly disgusting, of his sister Anna very likely still breeding away in Scranton.

Lost in such thoughts, they fell comfortably asleep; next day all was as it had always been before.

*

One night he went out to catch nightcrawlers to fish with. They were nightcrawlers because they came out at night, especially after it rained, like tonight. They were wriggling on the ground but they sucked back into it if he did not pick them up fast and hard enough. They were all over the yard.

Now, as he walked around catching worms to fish with, he heard a sound from near the milkhouse like something was hurt. And when he walked to the back of the milkhouse, he saw it was his sister Anna with one of her fellows on top of her. Some said she took after his mother, the way she looked, but he didn't think so. Her head was leaning back in the wet grass rolling back and forth with the eyes shut. Oh, it was strange the way she made the low sound, like she didn't even know it was coming out of her open mouth!

They were not very far from him, but they didn't see him. He had seen lots of animals doing it, lots of times, but he felt scared now all the same. Anna! he said out loud: Anna, your clothes are getting all muddy!

Anna opened her eyes, rolled them backward, and saw him. Teddy, she said, It's Teddy. And she started to hit her fellow on the back with her fists, and her fellow looked up and said to him, I'm going to kill you if you don't get out of here.

So he turned and jumped across the little brook beside the milkhouse, and ran out to the front pasture to catch more night crawlers. When he looked back at the yard again it was very far away, and his father was at the back door with a lamp. And try as he might, he could not hear what his father was calling.

*

Thing to do is go to the lunchroom late, one or so, read the paper and chew slow so you're the last one there and you pretty much know when all the rest of them've eaten. That way you don't end up having to clean the place up five, six times what with somebody coming late and leaving a pile of crap from his pail where you just been wiping or sweeping. You just empty the trash and wipe up the table and sweep. It's not too long if you just wait til everybody's done and once a week you have to get the vaccuum from supply and clean the floor good and mop it. They say for you to do the windows too but there's no use in that, it doesn't pay the time it takes and nobody notices. One thing, while you're waiting for them to eat you can keep a little something stashed in your pail so if old Binder walks in on you you can tell him you eat late and you're just finishing up. He won't care, see, if you sit down and rest a while as long as it's in the john in a stall out of sight.

*

Behind the desk Binder sat up straight and folded his hands with his thumbs pressed together pointing upwards. Now, what can I do for you? he asked, unsmiling.

Well sir, it's this leg of mine . . .

Ted felt foolish and defeated as he began to speak; but soon the pain formed the words. He let it talk. He heard himself tell the hard-looking young man across from him about the war, his convalescence, how sensitive his legs were, the way the pain never stopped, how it got worse all the time, how the legs could tell the difference in pain between rugs and concrete, soft and hardwood floors.

Binder didn't seem to be listening; carefully he filled and lit a large black pipe, and stared past Ted out the window at the shorn hills beyond.

Pain crept more openly into Ted's voice. He swung his leg up and planted his foot with a crash on the desk. Just look at his leg here, he said, rolling up his pants. Look at the color of that like it's dead, Mr. Binder, now isn't there some other job around here besides floor boy, be easier on this?

Binder leaned forward to look, and gave a low whistle. He settled back and scratched his armpit underneath his coat. I'm sorry, he said, I didn't know about this, uh, condition. You should've told me about it earlier. It's a problem now, you know, with the jacks. Now that they aren't logging any more, they want jobs here too.

Ted nodded. He was amazed he had said as much as he had, and he wasn't going to say any more. He took the leg off the desk. Binder seemed to be staring at his throat, and he wondered how the scars there looked now, how red.

They faced each other for a long time without speaking. Well okay, Binder said at last: I'll make you janitor for the john in plant one. Starting tomorrow. Just finish out floor boy today, okay?

He remembered all his life how tired and peeved Binder's voice sounded when he said that, and never forgot the good turn Binder had done him.

                                    *

That night after Virginia's visit to the doctor was the last potential disaster. What had happened, or, rather, what they understood of what had happened, they both promptly forgot.

Yet they were careful never to take the same risk again. For the risk was dread, an awful dread of finding themselves in a position where they would have to acknowledge what they had never got. Then, if that happened, they would be completely alone.

So, years later, when Virginia was told she had a bad heart, she hid her nitroglyne tablets in her mending basket and kept her broodings even from herself. And Brown, when she died, was equal to her. At the moment of her death, a spasm of grief coiled somewhere inside him, but cancelled itself immediately. When he did cry, months later, it was merely because he felt bewildered and a little sad, and he missed her around the house.

Her household duties, now fallen on him, went a long way toward diluting these feelings. Eventually he felt only a thick wistfulness on Sundays when he went to church alone. But whether it was because her support in their conspiracy was gone, or because he himself drew close to death, an old will began to stir in him again to find an absolute, something large enough to overwhelm his life. Each day from his black reclining chair he watched the quiz shows on tv, where random people won or lost their games with no discernible effort, no discernible sin. And the spectacle, these scenes of victory and defeat, blurred and clashed in his mind with the stark fragmentary moments his memory cast up. Questions formed: was there victory, had there been defeat? Had anything happened at all?

He felt the questions more than thought them, with a growing unease and excitement that only subsided when he remembered the job in the john. It answered no questions, explained not a thing. It was a constant only, empty of all value; yet still so strong and endless that it tended toward the ineffable, and drowned out other thoughts. Sometimes he concentrated on it so hard in that huge black chair, it filled his mind so full, that his lips would move as though they were trying to force out a message; but no sounds ever came out.

*

It was winter he liked going to church in best. Then they rode in the sled. The back of the front seat was the same as the back of the back seat, so Petey and he and Anna faced backwards and his mother and father, who drove, and Curt, they sat facing ahead. Nobody fussed or fought then because it was too cold; he pulled the horseblanket up to his eyes. It brushed against his black tie and made a crinkly noise. He and Anna and Petey pressed together and hoped the church would be all warmed up when they got there, and nobody talked up front either.

He liked to watch the two lines the sled sliced in the snow. He watched them so long after a while it was like he was on a magic sled that was going and going through the cold air and would never stop until it got to heaven.

*

1. Check Roll-A-Towel
2. Shitpaper
3. Soap
4. Mop floors (not too Wet)
5. Toilets and Urinals
6. Clean Lunchroom
7. Check Roll-A-Towel

8. Shitpaper
9. Soap
10. Mop floor (not too Wet)

Holding On

It was late July in the summer and he was thirty-two, past the age when most men of his kind had married, settled into their homes, and had children; but he had not. It had made him lonely and, until the loneliness sunk into him to stay, bitter and easy to anger. Once, drunk, he threw himself with an axe at the front porch of the farmhouse, so white and cool now beside the field. Then the next day he'd replaced the wounded boards. Long since, he'd stopped asking himself why he was holding on, and whether the shrinking farm was worth the factory job to keep the homestead twitching alive while he went numb and stupid packing ware that came to him down a belt. He knew he had made the decision very long ago and that it could not be taken back. So today he rolled it over in his mind only because what she had done to him, what they had done together, was a doubt sore in him that spread, making orneriness and questions. Nothing like it had ever happened before.

He was strong at thirty-two, as strong as he would ever be; now he carried two bales across the hill easily over to the haywagon, as easily as he'd done all day, at first when last night's booze sweated itself out of him, stinking, and now when you might suppose he'd be tired. He wasn't tired, though; it was Jack on the baler that was getting tired or lazy with the night coming on. And by the clear feel of the air and the look of the sky, blue all over, deepening in the valley below him to the east, he figured that the hay left could be baled and left til tomorrow on Monday. He could tell Jack to go on up the road home and leave the baler; no rain would fall and blacken the hay, probably, before he got out of the plant tomorrow to get the rest of it in the barn.

A little sweat stream rolled down his back as he walked across the hill, and hung on his lower spine. He scratched it off and wiped his hand on his dusty jeans, thinking. More than five hundred they had already put in today, and here was only forty, fifty left. It could be done, and he wanted it done; and not just for the pleasure of putting the last of the second cut in and having done with it, but also, especially, to make up for what went on between him and Lil last night, Saturday night. To balance that off.

So he called out to Jack, "Let's get the rest of it in," and Jack, old, red, wrinkled face scowled up, flapped his hand back at him and revved up the tractor. The baler filled the hill with its sound, like an insect breath and beating of wings, and the warm smell of the cut hay filled his nose. His hooks caught into two more bales, and he lifted and swung his heavy arms back and forth, letting them help him get to the wagon again; it would be done tonight and an end to it, to it and to last night too.

Was it her and Was she here. Those were the questions he had when he walked in the door and saw her in Tommy's, Lil Cranmer, all dressed up and drinking a glass in the place where he and those like him came for beer. Same face all right, her face like a wedge with the point down, nose pressed broad against her skull, but he would never have said anything even so, not with her in the outfit she had on. It was a sort of suit, very tight, the brown color of an apple cut and left out. Not if she hadn't said something first.

Why Luke Cavberg, what are you doing here? Throwing her hair she'd made blonde over her shoulder, acting like it was him that had come in the wrong place. Other fellows watched them. He could feel them thinking: there's Luke and Lil Cranmer together again, how about that.

Fifteen years since he'd seen her. Yes, a bunch of bad things must have happened to her to make her do that; even now, standing in the mown field feeling scared as hell of her in spite of knowing he wouldn't see her again, he felt sorry for what she must have been through since he saw her last.

Then he was mad again just as quickly, walking angry across the field, damning her. From where he stood in the field looking up it over the deep green trees, he watched the outlines of Jack's face moving against and across the sky as Jack rode over the field. And the anger in him settled again for a second on Jack, who had come this Sunday morning with the baler to help him get the hay in. At lunch they had sat under the nearest one of the soft maples between the house and the road to eat a sandwich, not wanting to go inside to the kitchen where the air was old and hot; and Jack, with his brown eyes squinting far off up the valley so as not to seem too personal, and giggling every so often his old man's giggle so as not to seem too serious, had started in again. Any other time wouldn't of been so bad. He would have nodded his head yes, it was a funny kind of a life to lead, and yes, he too supposed there was a girl around somewhere in these parts that could make a home again out of this place, and well, yes it needed some more life in it; he might have maybe hummed something to himself and said yes to all that as usual. But even in the shade of the maple, with the leaves at the top silvering with a little wind, he was greased with sweat like oil, the slow sweat of all that booze coming out on him, and his dink still seemed to ache.

And while Jack talked he kept remembering. The night before her mouth widened and shut a little while he was driving her car around and through the town. She said We've both learned to drink pretty well, haven't we? And he said Yeah we have; but it was a lie, he was drunk and he knew it. Drunk on his ass and trying to make believe it was the two of them still fifteen years younger, driving out to a back road to kiss and roll around. Back then they didn't talk to each other much either, and her face was still a sharp one then too, though not so much as now. Soon they were going together, and spending a lot of time at her house in town watching tv at night til her dad came home from working the 4 to 12, driving to Wilton to see a movie on the weekends. Fall of his senior year, he gave her his ring. One night in April that year they went up a back road into a hollow and up a hill, and parked beside a stand of hemlocks. After thirty minutes or so they got out of the car and walked out of the moonlight into the pines and did it. They kept coming back to the place all summer. One night as he lay on top of her and they moved together, a doe broke across the hill toward them. He heard the deer come close while he and Lil Cranmer did it and finally just caught a look at the doe's eyes glinting with moon, looking back at him before it jerked around and ran back toward the top of the hill. He'd had dreams about that night ever since. Like a stupid shit he kept thinking about that night all the while last night when he was drunk on his ass driving Lillian Cranmer around.

Oh, she must have known that he wanted to do it again as they used to, to get what they had back. So what happened was probably her way of telling him how it was between them, that those days were long-gone. He could understand that much of it, but it wasn't enough. Why did she have to do it that way?

Those were the things he was remembering and the thoughts he was having while Jack went on at lunch. He was angry and sick inside from thinking about it, and Jack still talking away how he too worked at the plant and tended a farm, with a wife and three kids, farm bigger than this one in fact, and it wasn't such a bad life, in fact it was a comfort . . . And all of a sudden he hated himself and Jack and Lil and the farm and the plant, hated everything so much his gut wrenched and heaved with it, and he told Jack to just shut his fucking mouth. Then Jack looked over at him, mouth full of sandwich, and said Okay you sonofabitch, and they sat there for about another fifteen minutes with only the leaves at the maples' tops making brushing noises and the drone of some locusts behind them in the woods.

Dammit, he wondered now, Can't that man go just a little faster? "Jack!" he yelled, and could hear, barely, his echo over the engine noise.

The tractor stopped. He saw Jack's head turn toward him; and then he wasn't mad any more. He had been all set to start yelling and now the anger was not there. But now Jack probably thought he was mad again, and was ready to get mad back at him. He had to say something.

"Think we got enough light left?" he said.

A dumb shit question; it didn't mean a thing. You could tell by the time it took Jack to answer he was expecting something smarter and worse. He could almost make out Jack's face squinching up, confused.

"Why sure," Jack said. "Huh-huh, hell yes."

He let Jack think whatever the hell he wanted to. Himself, he was getting behind in the loading. The next two he picked up he almost ran with over to the wagon, then trotted back to get two more. Let Jack and anybody else in the goddamn world think whatever they wanted to about him. They could do it for him. If they wanted to think he was lonely, all right, he was lonely, or crazy, or stupid. Holding on to the farm was none of their business; working at the plant was none of their goddamn business. They could judge him all they wanted. He was himself. It was the way he lived.

So you've been on the farm still, all this time, she said in Tommy's. He couldn't tell looking at her whether she was poking fun at him or not.

And working at the plant, he said.

Didn't you ever consider doing anything else? she said, and smiled at her glass.

Consider was a word that bothered him; she had picked that one up since he'd seen her last. It had nothing to do with anything they'd done together. No, he said. Never have.

She put her glass down and smiled across at him, except he could tell from her eyes it wasn't a smile really at all. Well, she said, I guess that's pretty admirable.

Admirable, he thought. He felt weak looking back at her, and ordered some whiskey.

The blood was pounding hard, almost hurting in his head from running and tossing the next bales up. He stopped and leaned against the oak bed of the wagon, wiping some sweat away from his eyes. The hay: he sucked in great smells of it as he caught his breath. It had been all the Cavberg farm was, that hay, twelve years or so now, since before the old man died. They'd sold all the rest of it bit by bit, the pasture, woods, cows, chickens; none of it would pay any more. The coops and stalls had rotted, and he bought his milk for the lunch-box thermos at the store in town and worked in the packing department at the plant. So it was only the hay that let him still call himself a farmer. It sold in the winter to the larger farmers, those rich and big enough to make a go of it, most of them down on the flats. He had no use for it any more, and yet it was his, grown from his land and on his wagon now. Just to grab and put it up against his nose, rough, prickly, and full of smell, made him feel some better.

Good enough, anyway, to think of her for the first time and just for a second without feeling mad or confused or sick as he walked back across the field. Ahead of him, Jack had just flicked the running lights on; it made him wonder if she would be still on the road to Albany now that it was getting dark. Strange to think of it, the car he drove last night in Albany now. He shoved away from the wagon and trotted over to pick up more, still thinking of that drive. For a while, he hadn't been wrong. For a while in the car they had been their old selves again. It was after she said they'd both learned to drink, hadn't they. You could feel it inside the car, the old comfort they'd built up between them, something worn and smooth as old leather. He kept sneaking looks at her. Yes, she was the same, Lillian Cranmer still. He was driving through the night in a car with her again; all could be as it was. Finally, his chest seemed to be swelling like something in there would make him start to cry in a minute. Then he spoke.

Lil?

Yeah?

When you went up to that secretary job in Rochester there at the end of that summer – how come you never wrote or came back, or asked me up?

She gave a nervous laugh. Oh, that's long-past, she said. What's it matter now?

I don't know, he said. I just always thought you would get in touch.

They crossed the river bridge without speaking. He didn't know why he had asked at all; now it wouldn't go away.

Did you start going with somebody else up there?

Aw, Luke, she said. Yes, eventually.

So there it was: eventually. It hadn't been somebody else right off, she just hadn't wanted to see him any more. He was silent driving then, with his mind asking questions, while she lit a cigarette. Parliaments; he'd seen the pack at Tommy's. When did she start smoking, he wondered. As soon as she left town? All the time they'd been together had she been waiting to be someone else, was she really someone else now? He was choked with his old need of her, and spoke again out of it.

Hey Lil.

Puffing on her Parliament. Mmm?

You remember that time we were in the pines and the deer came up to us?

Yeah, she said, you told me about it.

That was beauti – that was something, wasn't it.

Yes, Luke.

Boy, that was a beautiful deer.

Luke, she said quickly, in her other, hard voice like the way she talked in Tommy's, You know I never saw that deer.

Well it happened Lil, he said, jerking his hot face around. It really happened.

All right, she said. Carefully she grazed her cigarette on the edge of the ashtray until the bright edge fell off. But I didn't see it, she said.

That couldn't be so; she must have shared what he felt, must have gone through what he did back then. If she hadn't then there was another way for her to feel: that she was just something for him to do it on. And he couldn't let her think that. So he was glad he was sort of drunk; he could say what he had to. Still, he drew the back of his hand across his mouth and bit the skin on it before he spoke again.

Lil?

No answer. He looked over at her. She was looking straight ahead at the road when his words came out.

Lil, I don't know if you know this but I loved you back then. And I'm not sure of it but I think I still do. At least you're the girl I've thought about all these years.

No I'm not.

Quicker than scat she said it, in the hard voice. Then she turned and looked at him. I am sorry Luke, she said. But I really don't believe I am.

Not much use in saying anything else then. For maybe ten minutes they drove around. Before, he had been thinking of driving the car up the road to the hemlocks, but now there was no sense in it. He drove along, up and down the hills on the paved road outside of town, and what had been choked in him started to feel curdled and sour. He began to shake a little, and hated himself for his weakness in shaking. Finally he pulled over to the burm and turned around, spinning gravel from under the tires as he took off again.

Where are we going? she asked.

To get some more beer if it pleases you, he said, surprised at the anger surging up in his voice.

She looked over at him. He felt her eyes' soft look on him, and the flush in his face seemed to ease. It seemed like the night was inside his skull, moonlit and empty, full of small animal sounds, and he wanted her very much.

Luke, she said, as gently as if talking to a kid, Let's get it and go somewhere.

Okay, he said, Where to?

I don't care, she said. Wherever you want.

"Hook up now with the wagon?" Jack was up the field and across from him, with the tractor turned around so the head-lights were like two bright close stars. And here he was with a couple of bales in his hands, feeling lost, almost, in the middle of his own field. It was silly. Here he'd been standing with these bales and the moon already up, still daydreaming. Almost made you laugh.

"Sure, might's well," he called back to Jack, invisible behind the lights. Then he turned his face from the lights and walked again to the wagon. Of course she'd be in Albany now. He got two more bales on while Jack lined the tractor up with the wagon.

"You know," said Jack, stepping down off the tractor, "that's pretty good hay."

"Yeah," he said. "What with all that rain beginning of the month and all."

"Turned out good though," Jack said, and they both bent to pick up the wooden wagon tongue. He heard Jack grunt as they lifted, and had his bare arm scraped by the sweat-stiff sleeve of Jack's shirt.

"I'll hold it now," he said. "Go ahead and back it in."

He could feel the sweat breaking out on his forehead and his teeth gritting with the strain. The sound of the tractor when Jack turned it back on was terrific, like the loud uneven engine was inside his head. He did not watch Jack backing the few feet to the wagon tongue. He was staring straight down, eyes sting-ing, at the shaped wood lying across his arms. Damn woman, he was thinking. Damn her.

There hadn't been any way for things to go right by that time. A part of him knew that even before he had stopped the car, something in him scared and watchful in spite of the booze. But still he pulled onto the dirt road off the highway and drove it in silence, without glancing at her, up past the oaks and beeches to the hemlocks at the top of the hill where the logging trucks used to turn around with their loads. And when he stopped all he heard was the sound of his own short heavy breaths, as if he had been running; she was already out of the car.

She was ahead of him somewhere in the pines; he couldn't see her. He picked up his bottle of beer, took a long pull and put it back down on the hood; and a dizzy thought hit him: what if she wasn't here and he had just driven up drunk and alone? It seemed like he might have done that.

Lil?

I'm right here, she said, not thirty yards away.

Any other time you could have heard or seen any animal from that far, he thought suddenly. Then he stooped his head and put his arms in front of him like blind man's bluff, and walked into the dark beneath the trees.

She was sitting on the ground at the outer edge of the pines, looking down the hill to the hollows where a few barnyard lights glowed. She had drawn her knees up against her chest; as she rested her head on them, her face seemed not so hard, more like it used to be, like he remembered it. He kneeled down beside her, as close as he dared.

Here we are again, he said, but his whisper sounded way too loud. Where was the beer? he wondered.

She didn't act like she'd heard him. Instead, she pointed her hand at one set of the lights below. And that's the way the Cavberg place looks tonight too, probably, she said, not whispering, but right out loud in a false cheerful voice, worse even than her hard one.

No, not really, he said. Don't make no sense to have a light when all the stock's gone. He looked at his hands.

Aw Luke, she said. I'm sorry.

Sorry for what? he said. Nothing to be sorry about.

They didn't talk for a while. A little breeze riffled the needles above their heads. For some reason, he thought he would wait for it to die down, as if it would drown out his words if he didn't. His fingers felt numb. He rubbed them back and forth on his pants leg. Finally he said it anyway.

I always knew we'd be back here someday –

Is the house still the same? she said, quickly, loudly.

Pretty much, he said, and took a breath.

I should have known it would be, she said. You always did love old things so. I remember you showing me that old rocker of your great-grandmother's. I bet it's still there in the front room, still just the way it was . . .

Listen Lil, he said, you remember this spot all right. I know you do. This is where when you and I, when we lay together here, there was a deer came running right up to us and looked at us and then ran away. Dammit, you remember that. I know you do.

I don't, she whispered. She was crying. I don't remember that, she said. I'm a fool to come up here with you. Listen, Luke, you've –

He grabbed her shoulder and turned her by it and kissed her. Them his weight carried him and he was against and above her again.

In a minute, he raised his head and looked at her. Her eyes were closed and her face seemed sunken into itself, as if she were asleep. But she was crying. He could just make out the tears rolling from her eyes down the sides of her face.

Come on honey, it's all right, please honey, it's all right, come on, he said. It had to be all right. She turned her head to the side and stared across the ground, while he plucked with fingers shaking at the front buttons of her suit. He heard her sigh, like someone stretching to wake up, and then her very tired voice.

Oh Luke. Roll over, honey.

As he lay on his side, her hands traveled down his chest and stomach, unbuckled his belt, and unzipped him. Then she was touching him down there. The night air seemed so good and cool. She had a hold of him down there and was touching, up and down, so nice. They were almost together again.

He began to move onto her; she put a hand on his chest. Easy hon, she said, It's going to be all right this way, just take it easy. Her eyes were open now, burning back at him.

Stop then, he whispered. If it was not going to be right, the way it had been and was supposed to be, he didn't want it. But her fingers were right there, never stopping. He could not help it. Finally he shut his eyes and listened to the breeze in the pines. He was trying to bend it into the sound of deer legs running closer through the night while he and Lil . . . Then it was all wrong, and all over; and he turned his face from her and started to cry.

Why did you come back? he said when he could.

Because I wanted to, she said. And I thought – I thought I'd be safe now. I told myself it was pretty dumb of me to think you'd be here still expecting me. But I kept on thinking you would be, so I didn't come before now. Now I thought enough time surely must have gone by. And you were waiting after all, still talking about that deer. Old lover, old things . . .

Her voice was toneless and muffled, as if she were facing away from him too. He had just about stopped crying, and was buck-led back up again. He rolled over and up on his knees and looked at her as she looked down to the lights in the hollows; and anger streamed up in him. He grabbed her chin and swung her face around.

I bet you've pulled that little stunt before, what you did to me, he said, I just bet you have.

She opened her mouth to say something, still not looking.

Oh sweet Jesus, Lil, for God's sake, don't tell me, he said. I really honestly, don't want to know. Then he got to his feet even though he was again starting to cry.

"Got it?" he said.

Jack waved back at him; he eased off and dropped the iron fastening bit in. Then the two of them moved back to the center of the field, and picked up bales.

They worked that way silently for a while. Above the field the stars came out, and the moon, a little shrunken from the night before. The crickets started up, grew louder. Sometimes, in the stubble by his feet, he saw the green glow of a fire-fly. Inside him, hot breath rose and fell. His sweat cooled on his forehead, fell into his eyes. She was still in his mind, last night was still fresh. The pictures he had of them, in the bar, driving around, at the top of the hill, struck again and again and again. It had all still happened. She was gone. She had done what she did and left.

Jack's breath, when they met at the wagon, kept sounding shorter and raspier. Finally he saw him stumble a little with the heave up of the bale.

"Here, you're getting tired," he said.

He saw Jack's head turn to look at him straight on. "I'm just fine," Jack said. But he had a tough time getting the words out loud enough.

Old Jack, he thought, he's getting old. "Well, the pile's getting pretty high," he said. "Why don't you get on up there and I'll bring them over, and you stack them. There isn't that much more of it anyway."

So then again it was just him in the field. And what had happened, all of it, flashed and faded, and flashed again, as he carried the bales to the wagon. As he went back and forth, crossing the field to the wagon and back again, it all happened over and over. Her face, over and over, the cigarette in the ashtray, the trees over their heads, the lights in the valleys . . .

He turned and took her by the shoulder.

Old lover, old things, she said.

He took her by the shoulder.

She pointed at the lights.

His breath hushed in and out. The crickets cried out, and answered themselves. His swinging arms whistled through the air. She had been back, but was gone again. He picked up another bale. She had been back, and was gone. Back, and gone. Back, gone . . .

It was past when they brought it in the barn and walked away, both feeling queerly shy and full of satisfaction.

"Yes sir," said Jack, "yes sir, that's a good crop. Ought to be getting plenty for it come February."

"Well, thanks for the help," he said. He leaned against the rusted hitching post in front of the barn. "Get the baler up to you tomorrow after work. You want something to eat here now?"

"No, guess not. The wife, she'll be holding it for me."

"Give you a ride home then?"

"Sure."

Getting into the truck, a fine glowing tiredness gave him comfort. He looked over at Jack leaning back on the seat. "Thanks again for the help," he said. "Boy, sure is a relief to have it all in."

"Yeah, always is," Jack said.

"Working day shift tomorrow?" he said.

"Yeah, back on days."

"My turn to drive. I'll pick you up."

Jack nodded, and they were silent. Luke looked out at the fields they were driving past, smiled and smelled at the hay on them too, as if they were his yet. And from above and below the fields, over the sound of the truck on the dirt road, he heard the cries of peepers, cricket chirps, bird songs from back up in the trees. He sighed and rested his head against the seat. Of course there was a deer, he thought suddenly; and it seemed like he would see it right then, bright as day, if he could only close his eyes.

Fred Pfeil was born in Port Allegany, Pennsylvania and was educated at Amherst College and Stanford University. His short fiction has appeared in **The O'Henry Awards (1979)** collection. **The Georgia Review, The Sewanee Review, Ploughshares,** and many other periodicals. His first novel, **Goodman 20/20,** was published in 1986 by the Indiana University Press. He has taught Creative Writing and Literature at Stephens College, Oregon State University, and presently at Trinity College in Hartford, Connecticut and has participated in various movements for peace and social justice wherever he has lived and worked.